Secrets of Building a Million-Dollar Network Marketing Organization

from a Guy Who's

BEEN THERE DONE THAT

and Shows You How You Can Do It Too!

Dr. Joe Rubino

New Expanded Edition

Secrets of Building a Million-Dollar Network Marketing
Organization from a Guy Who's Been There Done That And
Shows You How You Can Do It Too.

Vision Works Publishing
Copyright © 2005
First edition copyright © 1997
By Dr. Joe Rubino
All rights reserved.
Published by Vision Works Publishing
P.O. Box 217
Boxford, MA 01921
(888) 821-3135 Fax: (630) 982-2134
www.cprsuccess.com
VisionWorksBooks@email.com

Manufactured in the United States of America.

Printed and published in the United States of America

ISBN 0-9728840-0-9
Library of Congress Catalog Card Number: 2003108211
10 9 8 7 6 5

Coming of Age

Network Marketing For The New Millennium

By Dr. Joe Rubino

With this book YOU will:

- Get the six keys that unlock the door to success in network marketing.
- Learn how to build your business free from doubt and fear.
- Discover how the way you listen has limited your success. And...
- Accomplish your goals in record time by shifting your "listening."
- Use the Zen of Prospecting to draw people to you like a magnet.
- Build rapport and find your prospect's hot buttons instantly.
- Pick the perfect prospecting approach for you.
- Turn any prospect's objection into the very reason they join.
- Identify your most productive prospecting sources. And...
- Win the numbers game of network marketing.
- Develop a step-by-step business plan that ensures your future.
- Design a "Single Daily Action" that increases your income 10 times.
- Rate yourself as a top sponsor and business partner.
- Create a passionate vision that guarantees your success.

And MORE!!

My object in life is to unite
My avocation with my vocation
As my two eyes make one in sight.
Only where love and need are one,
And the work is play for mortal stakes,
Is the deed ever really done
For Heaven and future's sakes.
—Robert Frost

Find a job you love and never work
another day in your life.
—Confucius

TABLE OF CONTENTS

Introduction

At some point in your network marketing career, you will be called upon to introduce a speaker at a meeting, training or company convention. I was taught a simple formula that works perfectly and I'll share it with you.

First, tell the audience what the speaker is going to tell them.

Next, explain why they should listen to him; tell them what gives the speaker the right to be there up on stage speaking.

Third, share a personal contribution the speaker has given you.

And finally – and for the first time – say the speaker's name.

I'm guessing I can use that same formula to introduce this book. So, here goes.

This book will actually show and tell you the secrets of building a million-dollar network marketing organization – no kidding!

I know that, because it's been written by a guy who really knows how to build a big business, because he's done it himself. And it's a powerful truth every successful network marketer recognizes: Once you've done it yourself – and only when you've done it yourself – you can teach others to do what you already know how to do.

I admire him for taking a number of principles and practices I hold in the very highest esteem – listening, vision, partnership and leadership – and bringing them down from the ivory tower of personal growth theory and making them pay and play in the real world of day-to-day business building.

My friends, I am pleased and proud to introduce you to Dr. Joe Rubino and his dynamite book, *Secrets of Building A Million-Dollar Network Marketing Organization from a Guy Who's Been There Done That and Shows You How You Can Do It, Too*.

There, that worked out pretty well.

In Secrets of Building A Million-Dollar Network Marketing Organization Joe can and does reveal the secrets he learned and used to build a million-dollar business – one that not only made Joe wealthy and successful, but created many happy, healthy, wealthy, and successful men and women throughout his network marketing organization.

Joe has truly *Been There and Done That*.

There are many books out there written by imposters, people who think or claim they know how to build a large, successful organization – but they've never actually done it.

Joe knows.

And because he does, he can show you too.

And it's not just the fact that Dr. Rubino has done it that's important – it's how he did it.

Joe's way has integrity. It honors people and their values. It's based in and on having a high-minded vision for people and their possibilities. It's got both head and heart – it's caring smart. It's all about offering partnership and being responsible for co-creating success with your people. It's about leadership.

It's about all these things, because they're what Joe's all about.

Joe's the best.

So's his book.

--John Milton Fogg
Author of *The Greatest Networker in the World* and
Conversations with The Greatest Networker in the World

Acknowledgments

This book is based upon my actual experience in building a large network marketing organization, as well as the many personal development and leadership concepts I learned from my mentors. Mike Smith of The Freedom Foundation, Carol McCall of The World Institute Group and Richard Brooke of High Performance People have all contributed greatly in the areas of listening, communication and values-based leadership. Smith, McCall and Brooke are pioneers in defining the new paradigm of network marketing, a paradigm that nurtures and honors both you and others. It's a win-win-win philosophy, in which choices are made only if they work for you and honor the other person and the world as well. Mike, Carol and Richard, through their respective companies, have inspired thousands to see what can be possible by valuing and listening to others. They have brought integrity and leadership to an industry in the midst of rapid and often turbulent transformation. Together with other MLM visionaries, they have done much to shift the dubious reputation earned by some of the predecessors in our industry. The leadership principles that these paradigm pioneers have taught serve as a role model for the new breed of MLM company which will be the norm in this new millennium. They have defined what the new network marketing company of the future will be based on: not just on better products or a better compensation plan, but better people.

Through the inspiration of leaders such as Brooke, McCall and Smith, network marketing will flourish far into the 21st century as a prime force for global change, which champions people, their dreams and positive visions.

To these leaders – and to all the others like them who will inspire millions to follow the path of heart in using the vehicle of network marketing to contribute their gifts to the world – I dedicate this book.

Further acknowledgments go to my two partners in life. First, my wife, Janice, whose support and understanding have made both my success as a network marketer, trainer, speaker, coach and this book possible.

The second is Dr. Tom Ventullo, my friend, co-creator of The Center for Personal Reinvention and my business partner in network marketing since 1991. It is through Tom's support, intuitive insights and partnership that I have been able to leverage my skills and effectiveness. And, special thanks go to Tom for his contribution to Chapter 8, on listening through objections.

Thanks, as well, to Dr. Ron Scheele for introducing me to this wonderful industry and for his mentoring, partnership, friendship and leadership. Ron is the definition of what a top network marketing leader can be.

Lastly, gratitude goes out to Bill DiPietro, Don and Mary Lou Vollmer, Anthony Stefanou, Khor Balsara, Gayle Driscoll, Greg McWatt, John Prange and to the thousands of visionary partners whose leadership is the source of my own success in this industry. Through each and everyone of these friends, business partners, mentors and team members, I've been able to compound my own individual efforts to offer the power of possibilities to the lives of countless others through the magic of networking.

Chapter One

Why Network Marketing...?

It's difficult to imagine that it's only been more than twelve years – my life as a network marketer, that is. In this incredibly short time, the events and experiences I've had, relationships I've developed, and personal growth I've witnessed in myself and others, seem more appropriate to 50 years or more in a normal person's life.

That's one of the great gifts of network marketing. In this business, it's possible to live a few short years filled with more rich adventures and special people than most people would experience in a lifetime.

An image I recently witnessed says it all for me.

Walking through a local zoo, I came across a gorilla sitting listlessly in his cage. This gorilla had lost all traces of energy and enthusiasm for life. He sat, in jail, in his own mess, the picture of resignation and despair. Although he was going through the motions of life, he had long since died inside.

The sight reminded me of the masses of people stuck in their self-imposed mental cages. People who, a little bit at a time, are losing their vitality and enthusiasm for life and work.

So many people are trapped in jobs they hate. Jobs that provide them with no sense of accomplishment, contribution, or challenge.

Like that poor gorilla, these individuals are so numbed by their situation that they fail to see any way out of a monotonous life that no longer meets their needs and wants, nor honors their values. They become resigned to an existence structured by those twin sacrifices: lack of money and lack of time.

Before long, that binding box they built begins to feel like home. Even the dream of a different and better lifestyle becomes remote, then fades and is forgotten forever. Their lives can often be summed up in one word – resignation. As Norman Cousins said, the tragedy of life is not death, but that which dies inside of us while we are still living.

As a general dentist in practice for 10 years, I had, not so long ago, lapsed into that kind of life's resignation. Although I was making a comfortable living, my income was earned day to day. If I worked my hours, like everyone else, I got paid. If not, I didn't. I resigned myself to the "fact" that dentistry was the only way I could earn a living. Though I enjoyed many aspects of my family practice, there was something missing.

Dentistry had become a job for me. Not a passion. I found myself looking forward to long weekends or those seven days of vacation that always seemed to arrive too slowly and pass by all too quickly.

Without realizing it, I had surrounded myself with a life driven by obligations. "Shoulds."
You know the ones. I should...

... go to work everyday.

... see those difficult patients who always ruin my day.

... do those procedures (like root-canals) that I found monotonous and unpleasant (not to mention painful for both patient and doctor!).

... do everything around the office myself (if I wanted it done right!).

... be responsible – the grand-daddy of all "shoulds."

Then came network marketing.

Networking provided me with a different and much more clear definition of what being responsible really means.

Responsibility is not burden nor fault. It does not involve blame and doesn't involve getting credit either. No shame and guilt. All of these things involve judgments and evaluations of good and bad, better and worse, right and wrong.

That is NOT responsibility!

Responsibility simply means "the ability to respond."

Responsibility starts with the willingness to deal with a situation from the point of view that you are both the architect and builder of who you are, what you do, and what you have! It means taking the viewpoint that you are the one "responsible" for everything that shows up around you in life. It's your creation.

This is the essence of what network marketing is all about – creativity.

It is about designing your ideal life. It's about first choosing all the elements of such a life, and then making them happen. Responsibility is the opposite of living out of mere knee-jerk reaction to the happenings of your world. True responsibility is possible only when you have the ability to knowingly choose your own actions.

Network marketing is simply the vehicle to live a life of choice. The financial freedom that can be created through MLM can bring about the personal freedom to live with complete responsibility, to create a life totally consistent with your values, goals, and dreams – and to have fun doing it, too.

Contrast that with how the majority of people you know now live:

Do you see resignation in their lives?

How many of them are living in hidden desperation?

Some Sobering Stats

In a survey of people between the ages of 45 and 64, conducted by the financial firm of Merrill Lynch, the following facts were revealed:

- 53% of the people wanted to retire before age 65.
- 74% expected the same or better standard of living.
- Women earned only 70% of what men do – and live longer.
- 59% expected most of their retirement income to come from Social Security.

- Baby boomers expected to live to age 85.

And more,

- The life savings of the average 50 year old is $2,500.
- The maximum Social Security benefit is $21,000 per year.
- Fewer people are worth $100,000 at age 68, than at age 18.
- Less than 1/2 of 1% of all Americans retire financially free.

Winston Churchill said that once – perhaps twice, but no more – in an entire lifetime will a person have an opportunity of life-changing magnitude. When such an opportunity knocks, it's up to you to accept it and make the most of it – or to simply let it pass by.

But the world that Sir Winston knew did not have network marketing!

As we enter the 21st century, these potentially life-altering opportunities are presented to people much more often than just once or twice in a lifetime – thanks to network marketing.

Networking presents the awesome power of possibilities to more people than has ever been available before. Each network opportunity possesses the potential for so many rich relationships and exciting experiences – chances to live a life of choice and freedom.

Each networking company's product line and opportunity is merely an avenue for discovery – the means for you to take control of your future and design it to meet all your needs. A way for you to live a life that honors your values.

Network marketing was founded upon the concept of

sharing great products with others. In the 1950's and '60's, the marketing spotlight was focused solely on the products themselves. Sales techniques were aimed at convincing customers of the value of a particular product after explaining all of its features and benefits.

Show and tell was what it was. Everything was product, product, product: new and improved products, hot products, breakthrough products! Show the product. Tell the story.

This basic show-and-tell technique worked great in the product-oriented past when there were only a few thousand products in the whole world a consumer could buy. But today, there are tens of thousands. Thousands of new (and improved, hot, breakthrough...) products are introduced every year, and 98 percent of them fail!

Can you see why, today, the focus cannot be on the products?

Sure, there have to be great products – and there usually are.

Sure, those products must give great benefits – positive results that enhance the consumer's quality of life – and they usually do. But there's more-much more.

And the more is – people.

Network marketing is about people.

At its best, network marketing is about people getting control of their lives, following their dreams, living their values, AND supporting others to do the same.

That's why traditional sales people often fail miserably in MLM. They're so indoctrinated in product, product, product, they lose sight of people, people, PEOPLE! Their focus is in the wrong place – either on the products, or on making themselves a lot of money selling the products. Neither of those reasons are very important to anyone else in the world.

What IS important to everyone in the world is relationships.

And network marketing is about relationships. Period.

That's why the old recruiting theory of "throw enough mud (i.e., people) against the wall and see what sticks" simply does not work. MLM is not about other people doing it alone and making you a lot of money. Rather, it's about YOU partnering with others to help them realize their dreams. And, it's about those people partnering with more "others" to help them realize their dreams, and so on.

Network marketing is about committing to the success of other people – to the same extent that they are willing to commit to their own success. That's where the power of possibilities in MLM lies! In relationships – emotional, committed, contributing, empowering, relationships. And whatever it is you contribute to others will come back to you ten-fold – minimum!

So, with this in mind, you can see that the successful networking distributor must be a person who has highly developed listening skills.

Listening to what others say, and to what they do not say.

Listening for what it's like to walk a mile in the other person's moccasins.

Listening for what's important to that person and what's missing in his or her life.

Listening for an opportunity to provide something of value to that person. To contribute. Make a difference.

Listening is the key!

A 30-minute monologue on the value of your product line, or on how great the company is, or on what you are doing in your business, is totally irrelevant. Who cares?

I know one person who doesn't care – your prospect! He or she cares about what's important to him or her. Not about you. And you will never know what's important to other people if your focus remains on yourself. Listening – not speaking – is the key.

Throughout this book, you will find that listening is a common thread.

Listen to your prospect.

Listen to what's important and what works for the other guy.

Listen to what the world is calling for.

Listen to yourself, and to how others are listening to you.

Listen to what's missing.

Listen and fine-tune your actions in each of those areas.

Listen your way to success!

Listening is necessary for effective communication. Communication is the foundation of all effective and rewarding relationships. And relationships are the key to success in network marketing!

All productivity (in life and work) takes place against a background of relationships. As you develop mutual interests, rapport, and a common purpose with others, awesome possibilities open up. That's the reason I consistently focus on relationships first. When positive results are lacking, I always look at the relationships to see "What's missing?"

You must constantly return to relationship-building. Too often, people see it as a waste of time, preferring instead to pursue only what they want for themselves from the conversation. Their impatience for "getting to it" and sharing their opinions is usually the source of their downfall.

People will not be willing to hear what you have to say unless they have an equal opportunity to make themselves heard. And who do you suppose comes first? Them or us? Only after they are heard will they decide to give you a chance to share with them.

So, if as I've said, relationships are the key to success in network marketing, what are the key relationships that contain the awesome power of possibilities for your success?

Number one is *Prospecting*.

Chapter Two

Prospecting For Aces

Like the prospectors in search of gold during the mid-19th century, today's networkers are attracted to the activity of prospecting with visions of striking it rich. And like those prospectors of old, the reason to play the game lies in its potential possibilities – those rich rewards.

Those old-fashioned prospectors had no certainty of success on any given day or in any particular mine or stream. Their techniques were crude, slow and labor intensive. While a few did hit it rich, most were left with shattered dreams and little to show for all their hard work and the often life-threatening risks involved in searching for gold.

Contrast this with today's modern mining. We use technology to show the presence of a definitive vein of gold. We have the heavy-duty mining equipment to get to the gold no matter where it's hidden, in record time, and cost-effectively remove it for a fabulous profit.

This book will, like modern mining methods, enable you to utilize the most powerful and effective technologies to leverage your efforts. Now you can replace the forty-niner's tin pan and pick-ax with your own version of a hi-tech, computerized earth-mover. And you'll be able to quickly locate where the gold (your future networking leaders) lies hidden before harvesting your find with newly developed skill and effectiveness.

Before we can examine the keys to successful prospecting, let's take a look at the prospecting paradigm that already exists.

By "paradigm," I'm referring to the common belief of what is true that's taken for granted by society or our culture.

For example: Go back before the time of Columbus. What was the paradigm – what was thought to be "true" by society – about the shape of the Earth?

Flat.

Was it true...?

As it turns out, no, but that's what the majority of society thought at the time.

It's important to pay attention to prevailing paradigms, whether they are "true" or not. Remember, you are almost always speaking and listening directly into these beliefs and expectations as you prospect for people to join you in your networking opportunity.

The Forty Year Career Plan

Now, for the majority of your prospects, there exists a paradigm called the "forty-year career plan." This plan is based on the following well-established logic:

You go to high school, study hard, get good grades, and are accepted into a good college. There you study hard, too, get good grades, which allows you to graduate with a good grade point average, as high up in your class as possible. Your good GPA and class-standing gets you hired by a good company that pays you a good salary, offers you good benefits, and lets you slip away for two or three good weeks of vacation each year.

This is good.

You work hard for the next 40 years (excepting an occasional three-day weekend, holiday and those two or three weeks each year when you "get away from it all"). After 40 years, you earn the right to retire. The good company that hired you right out of college looks at your years of good service and provides you with a good pension – augmented, of course, by your Social Security check, which is good.

You hope that's enough to live on until your death, or, if you are one of the thrifty, fortunate few, it might even be enough to let you live in the sun for a couple of months each winter, which is very good.

Sadly, less than one-half of one percent (.005) of all Americans end up financially free at age 65. In fact, most people are living on a small fixed-income with no more than a few hundred dollars left after paying their essential bills. That's just "the way it is," something those hard-working people are helpless to change – unless of course they hit the lottery.

Now, picture yourself approaching your prospect who sees the world through this firmly-rooted paradigm. You're enthusiastically talking of early retirement, financial freedom, and living a life of choice.

And what is your prospect hearing...?

Pie-in-the-sky lies. False promises. Fairy tales.

Think about it: in most cases, the awesome power of possibility you're offering – the chance to earn extraordinary monthly incomes and retire after only a few years of effort – is simply not believable at all! And what kind of person would say such unbelievable things?

Can you see what's happening here from your prospect's point of view?

Before you even think about sharing any of the potential rewards of your opportunity, you'll need to change that "40-year career plan" paradigm and demonstrate to your prospects that what you are saying is truly possible for them. And, you'll have to do it in a way they will truly believe.

How...?

The First Challenge

As you prepare to prospect, the first challenge you'll probably need to overcome is your own discomfort with the prospecting process.

It's understandable that most new network marketers will have some apprehension about introducing someone to a company's product line or opportunity. This awkward or uncomfortable feeling is to be expected with any new venture or activity.

Think back to your first date... first dance... first kiss.... Remember how nervous and uncertain you felt? Those feelings often accompany a new activity, just because it is new.

You probably felt the same sensations of nervousness or being ill-at-ease when you were first learning to drive. Remember how awkward that experience seemed?

Imagine your hands gripping the steering wheel at the 10 to 2 positions. Your seatbelt, cumbersome yet carefully fastened. You would check and double check all controls, lights, mirrors, gears. The radio had to be off, so as not to cause you distraction. You'd signal, look both ways, pull slowly into the street, and plod down the road, knifing through the wind at 10 m.p.h., just waiting for something – everything – to go wrong.

Now, recall your most recent merge up the exit ramp of the highway: 50, 60, 70 m.p.h. A Big Mac in one hand. A Coke in the other. Stereo blaring. Steering with two fingers and one knee!

Prospecting is just the same. Practice will help increase your confidence level. Every prospecting conversation can be an improvement over the last one – if you set out to accomplish it that way. Competence creates confidence. Those beginning fears will soon dissolve into the comfort of a well-known routine, as you begin to trust yourself.

So, how do you cultivate such self-trust?

By...

Creating a Vision Greater Than Your Fears

Have you ever looked in your rear-view mirror and seen flashing lights coming up behind you? Did you have that sinking-sick feeling in the pit of your stomach as you pulled over? Were your hands cold and clammy... and did your voice tremble a little as you managed a weak smile saying, "Hello, Officer. Is something wrong?"

Are these similar sensations to what you experience when you pick up the telephone to tell someone new about your opportunity? If so, you've got to overcome those fears before you can be powerful in your communications and attractive to others as a prospective business partner.

Fear paralyzes people.

We're all concerned to some extent with what others will think when we make our presentation.

Will I look bad?

Will people like me?

What objections will they have?

Will I be bothering them?

Am I trying to get them to do something they don't want to do?

Whatever your concerns may be, unless your focus is on something greater than your own anxiety, you face being ineffective and even immobilized by your fears. So, what's the solution?

Simple really. Create a compelling enough reason to act that outweighs your fears. When your "why" or reason for being involved in network marketing is strong enough, your fears will pale in comparison.

So, how do you create and strengthen that vision of yours?

Start With Identifying Your Passion.

By passion, I'm referring here to the "juice" that makes your life worthwhile.

Look and see if there's a common thread running through the activities you enjoy most. Make a list of all of your favorite things to do, hobbies, sports and recreations.

Ask yourself:

What is it I like best about doing this?

What values am I experiencing and expressing when I'm doing this?

(Examples of values might be: humor, independence, creativity, contribution, fun, freedom, adventure, intimacy, power, belonging, success or communication – to name just a few.) Look for the common themes that are important and valuable for you.

For me, creativity is a high-priority value. I really enjoy brainstorming, looking for possibilities, discovering new and exciting ways to approach each unique situation. I am most alive and engaged when I'm in that creative mode.

Also, I love to inspire others to see new possibilities for themselves, instead of dwelling on the problems and pitfalls in their lives. So my passion can be summed up as, "Inspiring the awesome power of possibilities in others through creativity." That's what gets me out of bed in the morning and fuels me to continue day after day, with real excitement!

That's Passion.

As you work to identify what it is that you're passionate about, keep looking for that underlying value or common thread that makes it all worthwhile for you.

If you like to play golf, go white-water rafting and hike, ask yourself: "What common element or value do I get from each activity?"

Perhaps you like the challenge of golf or the success that comes from getting better and better at the game. Maybe it's the thrill of rafting and the adventure of hiking.

You might then sum up your passion as "the thrill and adventure of pursuing the challenge of success."

Again, look for the values that you're experiencing and expressing – and those which are actually "being honored" – in each one of your passions.

Create a Vision of a Life Filled with Passion

With a focus on your passions and most important values, spell out your vision for your life. Be clear, specific, and detailed as you include such elements as where you'll live, what you'll own, who you will be with, what you'll be doing, etc.

Include as much picture-like detail as possible as if it was a movie. Create a vivid mental image of every important aspect of your life. And make sure to show how your vision is an expression of your passions and your values.

Look at this vision you're creating as a game you're playing – a game where you're designing your ideal life. To be truly powerful, create your vision as something that is much greater than about just you alone... something you can't do on your own... something that must involve and positively affect the lives of many, many others.

Include how you will contribute to the lives of all those people.

One way to get a clear picture of this is to ask yourself, "When I'm earning $X and all of my material needs and wants have been satisfied, how will I live my life...? What will I be doing...? What would make my life really worth living if I had the next 300 years to live it...?"

Now, write it all down.

Here are the key elements of a powerful vision:

ABOUT YOU

Who will you be?

What qualities will characterize you?

What will you do?

Who will you do it with?

What will you have in terms of both possessions (material needs, things and toys) and non-physical qualities (emotions, feelings, accomplishments – such as time freedom, peace of mind, fun, a sense of fulfillment, creativity, etc.)?

ABOUT OTHERS

To whom will you contribute?

How will you contribute to them?
In what ways will your contribution affect the lives of others? and...

What values will you honor-for yourself and others-through the fulfillment of your vision?

EXAMPLES of values:

contribution	happiness	peace
security	freedom	adventure
creativity	love	joy
belonging	excitement	recognition

Adapted from Richard Brooke's Vision Workshop

The notion of creating your vision was first introduced to me at a "Vision Workshop," conducted by network marketing visionary, Richard Brooke. According to Brooke, vision is at the very core of both leadership and success in life. It is essential that you first define your own personal vision in the most exacting detail. When your vision is explicit, written down, and reviewed daily, you will actually incorporate it into your life and work naturally and automatically.

And – this is very important! – you cannot live or become what you do not clearly envision!

One more important point about your vision: your vision must be created as an already accomplished reality. If you state your vision as something you want or desire, that is precisely what will manifest – you wanting, desiring your vision. If your vision is something you truly dream of having, shift your vision to having it, not wanting it.

Now, having a written vision and reviewing it daily is not enough. You must speak your vision. Without speaking it for all to hear, your vision inspires no one else. And for vision to take hold and grow into reality, it must be fed and fueled by inspiring others.

As you communicate your vision, new possibilities will open up for other people. **It is this quality of a vision being contagious that actually helps to bring your vision about and spurs others to join in bringing it about with you.** As you speak your vision, you project an energy that inspires others to create their own visions in partnership with you and yours.

The continual process of individuals creating, clarifying, and sharing their visions fuels the process for everyone.

Vision is always about partnership with others. In this way, a single powerful vision can be the inspiration for leadership that can bring about global transformation, as the vision spreads and grows in scope, strength and power. Vision is the fuel that drives the engine of change, growth, and the awesome power of possibilities in our world. What's more, there is nothing I know of that can move an entire room full of people faster or more powerfully than when each person shares her and his vision. You cannot help but be inspired by people's visions. Sharing your vision is a truly moving experience.

A network marketing organization without a clear vision is one lacking leadership. Without vision, there can be no leader.

Leadership, like vision, is synonymous with empowerment. *(Inspiration, after all, is the most empowering thing of all.)* Without these qualities as a foundation, any networking organization or company will have difficulty overcoming the obstacles which will challenge its existence. Focusing on developing leaders who are inspired by a common vision, which will nourish commitment to the success of others, will create success for you.

As an example, here's my vision:

It is September 21, 2016. My wife, Janice, and I are celebrating my 60th birthday at our winter estate in Hana, on the island of Maui, Hawaii, by hosting a party attended by a thousand of our closest friends. Our waterfront property spans several acres marked by waterfalls and lush greenery, home to hundreds of magnificent tropical birds. All our family and the close friends we've made over the past 40 years are here. Our friends look to our Hawaiian home as a place for them to relax, rest and recharge their bodies, minds and souls. Our doors are always open. We enjoy each other's company all year long during their frequent visits. We divide our time between our winter home in Maui and our spring, summer and autumn homes in the scenic White Mountains of New Hampshire, and the wonderful woods of rural Massachusetts.

Our lives have become totally devoted to contributing to others and discovering more about accessing our personal magnificence. Our network marketing organization consists of 1 million empowered leaders who are committed to championing others to be financially free, healthy and fulfilled in their lives. We have achieved the position of Intergalactic Director with 10 million in monthly volume and 12 strong front-line leaders.

Our company, The Center For Personal Reinvention, has impacted millions of people to live rewarding lives based on choice, contribution and empowerment. People hold the center as one of the foremost organizations in the world that supports people to live lives that work optimally, in peace, harmony and happiness. We spend a large amount of time speaking, writing, coaching and inspiring others to live lives of possibility. Our goal is to kill off the resignation that consumes all too many people's lives.

My book, "The Magic Lantern: A Fable About Leadership, Personal Excellence and Empowerment", first published in 2001, just sold 20 million copies! People have found it to be a window to realize life-changing insights. The book's tale of the secrets to achieving world peace through the creation of empowering interpretations has taken hold. The thousand years of peace it foretold of is well underway.

My "Power To Succeed" book series is recognized as the catalyst that has brought the personal development conversation into millions of homes. Millions have implemented its principles into their lives. It sets the new standard for creating effective communication and relationships that thrive. My book, "Restore Your Magnificence" has supported millions of people to realize their God-given magnificence and live empowered lives, fueled by their passions and sourced by their life purposes.

My focus, now, is on continuing personal development, both for myself and for others. I continue to champion people around the world to maximize their effectiveness, happiness and power through my public speaking engagements, transformational courses, personal coaching and writing. I am humbled by the thousands of people who have stepped forward to join us in our vision of impacting people's lives. We now work in partnership with these friends to honor our values of contribution, belonging, adventure, abundance and fun!

People the world over have learned to see networking as synonymous with contribution to others and personal growth. My story, featured on the covers of Success and Time Magazine, has inspired thousands to live their lives full out and with passion. We have contributed to shifting the old paradigm of struggle, suffering and resignation.

Thanks to our efforts, people around the world believe in themselves and in their ability to contribute to others. Third World countries raise billions of dollars yearly through networking enterprises patterned after my charitable programs. Due to the elevated levels of self-esteem of so many, wars are now a thing of the past. People everywhere have embraced the new paradigm of living in harmony, love, abundance and contribution to their fellow man and woman.

We are in excellent physical health. We have abundant rich relationships. We devote time daily to our personal and spiritual development. Money is no object for us. We have all of the cars, toys and other possessions we could ever want. A large portion of the income that our organizations produce is used to fund our global humanitarian projects. We have more than enough money to support the dozens of worthwhile causes we're passionate about. Among these is quality education for all children, programs that champion the magnificence of kids all over the world and support people seeking to better themselves.

We travel the world extensively, visiting every continent and country we've ever had an interest in exploring. Many of our partners have taken on similarly rewarding lifestyles fueled by their passions. We've made friends everywhere we've traveled and have lived our lives as a daring adventure, always in search of the awesome power of possibilities.

As you can see, my vision is clear, detailed, complete, and includes both how my values are expressed and how I see myself as a contribution to others. It motivates me with a vivid picture of the results of the game I plan to play for the next several years and is fueled by the empowering emotional energy of my passion.

And... I speak it all the time!

Please, make time right now to write out your vision for the next five years.

Use the following questions to help stimulate your imagination to make your vision as rich and detailed as possible.

Do not continue reading until you've done this!

CREATING YOUR VISION

1) What will you have?

2) Where will you live? With whom?

3) What kind of house, cars, and possessions will you have?

4) What will you earn?

5) What will every aspect of your life look like?

6) What will you do?

7) What hobbies will you pursue?

8) Will you travel?

9) How would your ideal day be spent?

10) Who will you be? For what qualities will you be known?

11) What impact will you have on others and the world?

12) Who will you contribute to and how?

13) What legacy will you leave behind?

14) If all of your finances and day-to-day challenges were handled, what would you do?

15) How would you choose to live the next 100 years of your life, if you could?

There are several reasons for taking the time and effort to create this vivid picture of your future.

First, doing so sets into motion unconscious forces which work toward accomplishing the vision. The reason this works is that the human mind cannot distinguish between an image that is real and one that is simply vividly imagined. By clearly defining your vision and keeping it in front of you daily, it will live in your mind as a positive accomplishment, something you expect will happen because, in your mind, it already has!

This will prompt you to look for, be open to, and explore the awesome possibilities which would have gone by unnoticed without such a clear mental picture in place.

By creating such a positive expectation, your mind generates actions that are consistent with that image. This occurs whenever your image of the future is higher than your current situation. Your expectations provide motivation to shape the future for yourself.

In contrast, if your expectation for the future matches your current situation, there is little motivation to better your circumstances. That condition can be described as apathy, and being apathetic all but guarantees you'll maintain the status quo. Another word for this condition is res-ignation.

If you expect a future that's lower than your current sit-uation, that unconscious negative motivation promotes self-sabotaging behavior.

Take the example of a young golfer who finds herself up by ten strokes over the seasoned professional after nine holes. If that golfer expects to lose – because she doesn't deserve to win, is too young, or because she is way out of her league – her subconscious will negatively affect her play, causing her to "choke." The self-defeating behavior becomes a self-fulfilling prophecy. That young golfer plays a match consistent with the image she holds of her posi-tion or skill.

Have you ever seen a similar situation in sports before...?

Remember...

IF YOUR FUTURE EXPECTATION is higher than your current reality, it creates motivation.

IF YOUR FUTURE EXPECTATION is the same as your current reality, it creates apathy.

IF YOUR FUTURE EXPECTATION is lower than your current reality, it creates failure.

WHAT YOU EXPECT IS WHAT YOU GET !

This is the first reason to create a powerful, positive expectation or vision of what lies ahead. The second reason has to do with the power a positive vision has to fuel commitment and overcome temporary obstacles in the way of its accomplishment. (For more extensive treatment on this subject, look for Richard Brooke's new book, *Mach II with Your Hair on Fire*)

I talked about how prospecting and building a business in network marketing is often uncomfortable at first. For many, it's downright scary! This fear literally paralyzes some people. So you need to have something stronger than your fear to keep you on track and in action.

Let me give you an example.

If I offered you $10,000 to walk across a 20-foot steel beam laid across the floor of your living room, would you do it? Of course you would! There's plenty to gain – $10,000! – and little to lose – a misstep will merely have you standing on the floor.

Now, what if I offered you the same $10,000, but this time, the beam was suspended between the tops of two 48 story skyscrapers on a windy day – in the rain...? You wouldn't risk it, would you? The potential gain ($10,000 in cash) does not outweigh the potential risk (death).

Let's take a third example where the same beam is suspended between the skyscrapers, but this time your four-year-old child is at one end atop a burning building. The only way to save him is to go across that beam. Would you do it?

Of course you would! I didn't ask if you'd like to, or if you'd think it was fun. But you would find a way, because your reason or "why" is worth the downside potential of falling off. Your actions are consistent with what's at stake.

You can harness that same powerful motivation in creating your vision for the future. If you are really clear on "why" you are involved with your MLM company, if this vision of your impact on your own life as well as on the lives of hundreds, even thousands of others is clear, all fears or stops will look trivial by comparison. It will be as if you were simply crossing a beam lying on your living room floor.

So, let your vision be the ideal result of the game you're about to play for the next few years. Make sure it's powerfully tied into your passion and a reflection of the ideals and values you treasure most. With such a potent image to motivate you, few things will be able to derail you.

Now, let's look at some of the essential elements for your prospecting success.

Chapter Three

Prospecting Is a Numbers Game...
Or Is It?

Have you heard this before:

"It's only a numbers game.
If you speak to enough people, you're guaranteed to succeed."

While the vast majority of distributors fail because they don't speak with enough people, success through numbers is only half true.

Prospecting is a numbers game to this extent: If you don't speak to enough people, you can't possibly win!

Yet there are other, all-important aspects to prospecting.

How good are you at listening for what's important or missing in that person's life?

Are you able to create enough value to get your prospect's full attention?

How attractive are you as a potential business partner and sponsor?

Let's consider the numbers aspect first. How do you know how many people are enough?

Well, that depends upon your goals and your ratios.

By goals, I mean how many people you want to bring into your business. Your goal must be grounded in your ability to take the actions required to accomplish that goal. In other words, your daily level of activity needs to be able to support your goals and expectations.

This is where ratios come in.

By ratios, I'm referring to the average number of prospects you will need to approach to put one person into your business. For many new distributors, this "approach" number may be fairly large – perhaps 20 or more. As a new distributor gains confidence and knowledge (remember when we spoke about self-trust?) and learns to recognize and communicate effectively with potential leaders, this number, and the accompanying ratio, will decrease.

So, let's say that you (as an average new distributor) need to speak to 20 prospects before one will agree to join your company. And let's go on to say that for every 10 new distributors, one will fit your definition of a leader out to build a large business in partnership with you. From these ratios, you can see that you would need to prospect 20 people to find one new distributor. And you would need to sort through 200 prospects in total to find your one leader. If your goal is to find one new leader per month, you had better be prepared to speak with about 200 people every 30 days to stay on track.

Ratios are intended to give you a starting point to judge the level of activity you will need to reach your goal. As your enrollment skills improve, your ratio will decrease, and you'll be speaking to less prospects, yet achieving the same result. Every month, keep a log quantifying your actions and results to see what your projected ratios will need to be for your next month's activity.

Now you have a place to start. You have an estimate of how many conversations you'll need to get going.

So, who will you talk to? Where are you going to get your prospects?

That's your next step.

Prospecting Sources

Traditional network marketing teaches us to construct our names or notification list based upon who we know in our circle of influence, or "warm market." This includes family, friends, acquaintances, associates and business contacts. In short, just about everyone you know or know of.

This is indeed a good place to start building your list. You can then "leapfrog" with these prospects to see who they know and use their referrals to further expand your list of prospecting names.

Another often-used technique to create a list of prospects is to use a memory jogger like the yellow pages. Ask yourself, "Who do I know who is an accountant, an architect, an attorney, ..." Think in terms of occupations and affiliations, always asking, "Who do I know who...?" Include all professional acquaintances, business sources, former school classmates, clubs (Toastmasters, Rotary, Lions, Elks, VFW, etc.). Include study clubs, church groups, networking groups, and all other organizations where people come together in community.

Now, this approach is a two-edged sword. Many distributors use this warm market list to attract powerful people with whom they have credibility. But the downside, for most people, is that until you have proven yourself successful in this business, it's often uncomfortable or distasteful to "hound" friends and relatives. Also, what do you do when you run out of your personal names list?

In addition to prospecting all those you know or interact with on a daily or weekly basis, several strategies exist to actively prospect different groups of people in a variety of proven ways.

Prospecting Your Niche Markets

As networkers, we are all more powerful with some people and in is some arenas more than others. Often times, success in building a prosperous network marketing business is greatly facilitated by identifying your own power niches.

Allow me to explain.

Developing commonality with others is one of the keys to developing rapport. And rapport is a critical element necessary if you are to be heard by your prospect. To the extent that your prospects "get" that you are interested in them and you have things in common with them, they are more likely to be willing to listen to what you have to say. So, to maximize this advantage from the start, why not seek out those individuals with whom you have one or more items in common.

Identify Areas Of Commonality

The following list can serve as a starting place to begin to explore those arenas in which you are likely to find others with common interests and backgrounds.

Make a list of as many prospects as possible with the following items in common:

profession
work background
religion
ethnic or racial group
club membership
school class
language
special interest or skill
common challenges
geographic location
childhood affiliation
mutual friends or acquaintances
family ties
favorite charity
political or other affiliation
parents with college tuition bills
people working two jobs
And, the list goes on and on.

The idea is to begin to look for those with whom you share some bond.

If you are a teacher, you know all of the challenges that teachers as a profession are likely to face. Identify why your opportunity would be appealing to teachers, gaining clarity on the specific benefits to teachers. Then go after this group, speaking your commitment to support teachers in becoming financially independent – to be able to teach out of choice because they love to rather than because they need to in order to survive, etc. The same principle applies to any niche market or group.

The network marketing company that I have been affiliated with for the past twelve years has seven different product lines that appeal to different niche markets. For example, with our oral health care line, we target dentists, hygienists and those concerned with maintaining optimum dental and periodontal health.

As a dentist (now retired), I decided to target this market. As a result, I focused on the benefits of my product line and opportunity as it relates to those in my profession. With this focus, I speak to dentists and hygienists of office wellness centers, the treatment of halitosis, periodontal management, secondary income streams in the practice, staff profit sharing programs, a colleague referral program, the tax advantages of a networking business, and practicing ideal dentistry out of choice instead of obligation. You get the idea. With this type of laser focus, I went after and attracted thousands of fellow dental professionals who shared similar challenges in their practices and their lives.

We did the same thing with our pet care product line, targeting veterinarians, groomers, veterinary technicians, and pet owners with all of the benefits of interest to these groups. Likewise, with our weight loss product line, we have successfully targeted both men and women with concerns about either losing those unwanted pounds or gaining more energy, a group that excludes very few. Our air purification line particularly targets realtors (who see great increases in home sales), pet owners, smokers, and others who wish to eliminate odors from their homes and offices while improving air quality. Each product line has particular appeal to a certain group of individuals. By focusing in on these markets, product interest and prospecting success dramatically increases.

The same concept applies to other areas of mutuality. If you speak French, target others who speak French. Let them know that you are seeking bilingual leaders. Advertise in French publications; seek out French speaking clubs and organizations. Go where you are likely to find your ideal prospect.

Do you have a favorite cause to support? Identify why others with your interest would want to join you in business and set a goal of speaking to 500 individuals with this focus over the next two to six months, depending upon your commitment to action. When you focus on whom you want to attract, they tend to show up in droves.

Create A Unique Selling Proposition Pertinent To Your Target Market

Begin by making a list of all of the features of your company, product lines and business plan that would be attractive to those you are targeting. The features are those items about you and your company, opportunity, products, compensation plan, etc.

Each feature provides your prospect with a certain benefit. It is these benefits that you will speak about to interest your prospects.

Benefits are about the prospect, something of value that's in it for them.

For example, your weight loss product may have xyz ingredients that make them unique or effective. The ingredients are features. The fact that the product can help your prospects lose weight or gain energy is an important benefit that would be of interest to them. Always speak in terms of benefits and support these benefits with features.

As you speak to more and more prospects in each niche market, you will gain more and more insight into the challenges, needs and desires of that group. This knowledge will assist you in continually tweaking your presentation to better hone in on what is of interest to them.

Speak To Your Niche's Concerns and Pain, Hopes and Dreams

Your effectiveness will come in identifying the "seeds of discontent" or what's not working in your prospects' lives for them. Whether it is too little time to spend with their families, not enough money to live the life they once dreamed of living, the stress of providing a quality education for their children or any other problem they are faced with solving, your job is to identify the pain in their lives and look with them to see if what you are offering might shift them out of the situation. When you are able to create an opening for them to see a possibility with your opportunity or product, you have taken the first step in creating an opening to be heard. With this knowledge, you can look to contribute to their lives, creating rich possibilities for them to step into. When you become adept at creating these rich possibilities for your niche group, you will find your business will begin to grow rapidly.

Depending upon your company's product line, your focus could be a generic one, such as targeting entrepreneurial individuals (i.e., anyone seeking an opportunity, which today means nearly everybody!). Or, if your products are appropriate for a specific group of people, you could use a more targeted approach, prospecting them as a group.

For example, if your company has a skin care line, you might direct your approach to cosmetologists, salon owners, estheticians, or women's organizations. Likewise, if your products are dental, automotive, pet-related, nutritional, or home-protective, you would prospect those people who have an affinity for your particular product line. Given this, it's especially valuable to enroll those professionals with credibility in a particular field who would personally use and recommend your products to others who respect their reputation.

More On Knowing What Makes Your Company Unique

What makes your company, product line, or opportunity special and attractive to your prospects?

Before you prospect person number one, you've got to develop a clear picture of what makes you and your opportunity unique and valuable for people. Write each point down clearly and succinctly so that you will be able to speak them to others effortlessly.

In our over-communicated society with nearly 8,000 advertising messages hitting people every single day, you must distinguish yourself and your products as attractive, unique and exciting to your market. When you speak about your company in such a clear and compelling way, people understand why you are unique and how special you are. It makes you stand out from the me-too crowd. At the same time, you can motivate your prospect's curiosity to find out more.

Examples of Unique, Concise Company Statements

Randy Gage, marketing guru extraordinaire, teaches of the importance of having a concise, hard-hitting "USP" or unique selling proposition. Your USP defines how you and your company are special and attractive to others within your target market. Your company may fit more that one description. In fact, the way you describe your company and opportunity must be tailored to the individuals you're approaching.

The following statements are all appropriate examples to give you an idea of what you can create for your unique company and product offering. Taylor the statement to match your company and opportunity's benefits. When I'm prospecting, I choose the one Company Statement that best fits what I perceive my specific prospect's core interests to be:

1. We are a health professional network that allows health experts, just like you, to create a second royalty-type income that can lead to early retirement.

2. We are a leadership development company recognized as a role model for the MLM industry, that supports people like you to develop lucrative second incomes.

3. We are a health and wealth company committed to contributing to people's health, longevity, and financial freedom. What do you do?

4. We are a cutting-edge nutritional product company committed to people's well-being. We're rapidly expanding and are seeking business partners now. Do you know anyone who may be interested in earning an extra $5,000 to $10,000 per month?

5. We are a professional home-based business opportunity that helps people leave the rat race behind. Do you know anyone who is unhappy with their current job?

6. We are a debt-free, stable, 13-year-old networking company committed to developing financially-free leaders in the world. Do you know anyone who might want to develop an additional royalty-type income?

7. We help people save money on their utility bills - guaranteed. Do you know anyone who would like to spend less on their phone, gas, electric or internet bills?

The list could go on and on depending on the variety of individuals I plan to prospect. The key is to interest people while, at the same time, creating an opening for them to have a conversation with you.

Now...

How to Use Your Company Statement When Prospecting

There will be occasions when you'll only have one or two minutes, or limited space, to present your company to people. This is where your Company Statement comes into play. Use it as a starting point until you are better able to explore what is important, of interest or concern to your prospect.

Alternative Prospecting Sources

Besides prospecting your warm market of friends, relatives, acquaintances and business associates, let's explore some additional options.

The traditional MLM philosophy was against using advertising to build a networking organization. It was thought that advertising was not easily duplicable, being both expensive and mostly unnecessary for networking-based MLM success.

Times have changed. The modern "heavy hitter" has learned to take advantage of a variety of advertising strategies, both traditional and online, to support a successful prospecting campaign.

For example, the formation of ad co-ops allows a number of individuals to collectively pool their funds, giving them leverage to purchase advertising that would be cost-prohibitive for any one or two of them alone. Also, the capacity of voice-mail systems to gather prospects' inquiries and redirect them to individual co-op participants has greatly simplified the distribution of qualified prospecting leads.

Three-way calling combined with teleconference bridging also allows an unlimited number of prospects to hear a presentation by a powerful speaker who can effectively do a long-distance presentation for a nearly unlimited number of prospects at one time!

Let's explore some of the different prospecting sources available to shift your prospecting into overdrive. But before we do, let's focus first on the all-important "headline" each will have.

Headlines

Headlines are critical. A compelling one will grab your reader and demand that he continue on to explore what you have to offer. A boring, un-enrolling headline will cause your reader to skip over your message and throw it right in the trash.

Headlines need to be benefit-driven. They must tell your prospects immediately that what follows can contribute to their lives in one way or another. A good headline will arouse curiosity, stimulate interest and demand that your prospect continue to find out more.

Most marketers miss the boat by having headlines that are feature-driven, that is, about the product, company or other trait of more interest to the advertiser than the prospect. Benefits are about your prospect and what they'll get. Features are about you. Too often your prospect will not be able to link your feature to a benefit they are interested in. So do it for them with a headline that shouts the benefits.

For example, the following are feature-driven headlines:

DEBT FREE Company Expands Nationwide

Solid Management Team Leads Company

10-year old company experiencing stellar growth

Our products are Alcohol-free

Each headline speaks about the company or product – not about the prospect. Contrast that with benefit-driven copy:

Have the Security of an

Income that will Last a Lifetime

Exit the Rat Race with a 6 Figure Dream Income

Come Grow with Us and Earn a Full-time income with a Part-time Effort

Have the Peace of Mind that You Won't get Cancer

These headlines offer benefits to your prospects and invite them to learn more. Now, let's look at some prospecting sources:

Direct mail

The most effective direct-mail campaigns are aimed at a particular, target market.

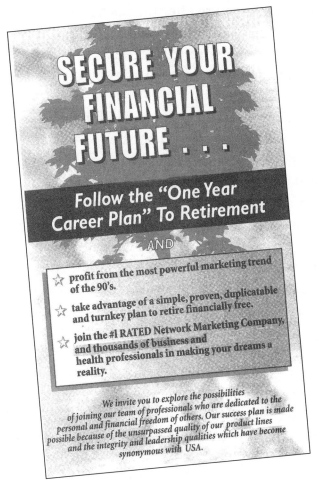

SECURE YOUR FINANCIAL FUTURE . . .

Follow the "One Year Career Plan" To Retirement

AND

☆ profit from the most powerful marketing trend of the 90's.

☆ take advantage of a simple, proven, duplicatable and turnkey plan to retire financially free.

☆ join the #1 RATED Network Marketing Company, and thousands of business and health professionals in making your dreams a reality.

We invite you to explore the possibilities of joining our team of professionals who are dedicated to the personal and financial freedom of others. Our success plan is made possible because of the unsurpassed quality of our product lines and the integrity and leadership qualities which have become synonymous with USA.

First step, you've got to determine the profile of your ideal prospect. Stand in his or her shoes and ask yourself what benefits would appeal to you about your company if you were the person being prospected. Design your direct mail piece to highlight those main points of interest.

Focus on the benefits – not the features.

A benefit is something that the prospect gets by joining your company. If you can't put "You get" in front of a statement about what you're offering, it's a feature – not a benefit. People are attracted to benefits – not features. The ability to clearly communicate benefits for your prospect separates an effective advertising piece from one that has little or no appeal.

Your mailing could be an eye-catching postcard, a hard-hitting multi-page letter, or a booklet or audio tape explaining why your opportunity is so hot. For the most part, keep it simple and direct, inviting and compelling. Again, design it to stimulate interest or arouse curiosity. It must leave your prospect hungry for more. For example, take a look at the "self-mailer" on page 61. It is benefit-driven, supported by features and makes a compelling argument for why someone would want to join our organization. When mailed to a good quality list, we consistently got a 3% to 4% response (excellent in direct mail) which was further improved upon with follow-up calls.

There are many companies that will sell – not just rent – you a direct mail list appropriate and specific for the market you have decided to target. Deal only with reputable companies offering fresh lists with guaranteed deliverable names.

The reason you want to buy the list is for the purpose of additional mailings. It's rare that people respond on the very first appeal. Often, it takes four or five contacts to produce an interested inquiry.

Even better are lists that also include phone numbers for those all-important follow-up calls. Such lists, though more expensive, will always ensure a better return giving you the option to follow up with your prospects by phone right after they receive your mailing.

With direct mail, the most logical targets are people directly related to your product line. For example, if you are marketing pet care products, you would mail to a list with a known interest in animals. Lists of "opportunity seekers" or known MLM participants are also available. Depending upon your offer, these may be very productive. But be aware that such lists are bound to contain many MLM "junkies" (they get into dozens of programs, one right after another, with loyalty to none), curiosity seekers, and other "marginal-quality" prospects who will reverse the prospecting process by trying to enroll you in their programs.

When doing a mailing from a list, it's a good idea to do a test mailing of between 500 and 1,000 pieces to discover your average response rate. If this test mailing proves successful, you can then mail in as massive quantities as you choose (and can afford) with a good prediction of what results you can expect.

Typical response rates for a compelling offer from a decent list will average two to three percent. Again, your success will dramatically improve when you follow up your mailing with a phone call.

Mailing lists vary tremendously in quality. For example, opportunity seeker lists with names that have been compiled more than 30 to 60 days ago, probably have lost much of their value as many of these people will have already found an opportunity.

Also, many lists are "oversold," some even to multiple distributors from the very same company!

Recently, a friend of mine purchased a year's supply of names of people who had attended an opportunity show in a different city each month of the year. This same list was sold to at least six distributors in her company, and for a hefty price at that! As a result, the list – a weak one to begin with – turned out to be a complete waste of time and money. Imagine, six different appeals, arriving days apart, and all for the same company....

The quality of the mailing list is essential to the success of your mailing!

So, let's assume you're able to find and purchase a quality list, with fresh names and few duplications, from a reputable list broker. How can you further increase the probability of a high response rate?

I've found that using a standard size #10 white envelope, hand-written, with a personal name on the return address works best.

Master marketer Randy Gage suggests you type, on the front of the envelope in capital letters "Critically Important" or "Urgent, Immediate Response Requested." Also, letters sent first class with a colorful stamp have a better (and more personal) look to them than typical junk mail sent in a mass mailing at a bulk, discount rate.

If you are following up an inquiry, it helps to remind people of the wording of the ad to which they responded, to refresh their memory and re-kindle their interest.

Another increasingly popular form of direct mail involves the mailing of an audio cassette tape targeted at a particular niche market. Several companies have grown exponentially simply by mass mailing of their audio tapes to hundreds of thousands of potential customers or distributors. Tape mailings have been extremely successful – either by targeting the network marketing/business opportunity community or by mailing to customers who have subscribed to a nutrition magazine or purchased a nutrition product in the past.

Success through tape mailing requires numbers. Those most successful mail to 50,000 or more names with the expectation of attracting a dozen or so "aces" who will go on to build a large organization. Of lesser importance but also valuable are the hundreds of product customers that typically result from a mailing.

Greg Arnold, author of *The Multi-Level Mangler in King Arthur's Court* is an expert in building an organization through cassette tapes. Greg has a set of five criteria he looks for in a successful tape. They are:

1. The tape has to be a bit on the controversial side, that is, it must raise some sensitive issues that compel the listener to action.

2. It must present information that is perceived as a breakthrough. It need not be new or unique necessarily but the perception must be that it is.

3. A tape utilizing fear of loss is much more motivating than one that only promises gain – and it must be backed up by strong compelling benefits. People must have concerns raised which motivate them toward a purchase of the product or entering into a program.

4. There must be the perception that the only legitimate, viable source of the product is with the company featured in the tape; and

5. The tape should end with a powerful call to action.

Using such a tape, Arnold did three mailings of 190,000, 120,000 and 250,000 cassettes over a six-month period, financing his mailings from an ever-growing co-op of distributors and investors pooling their resources. When the dust settled, at the end of eight months, he had sponsored 183 front line distributors and had amassed an organization of 5500 people in all. Thirteen out of the company's top 15 money earners were found in the mix providing Arnold with a monthly check in the $25,000 range.

Arnold shares the following insights about mailing tapes:

With a good tape you can expect about a 1% response when mailed to a cold market list. In contrast, when mailed to one's warm market the success jumps to about 8%. And to increase the response rate even more, he suggests calling your prospects first, getting their permission to send them the tape and their commitment that they will listen to it – and then follow up with another call 48 to 72 hours after they receive the audio tape.

With a consistent plan of mailings and follow-up calls a good tape sent to the right audience can produce an incredible source of leads. But remember, it still comes down to the enrollment skills of the networkers to convert these leads into productive and successful distributors. Even when done professionally and at its best, direct mail may be less cost-effective than several of the other alternative modes of advertising.

Card Decks and Bulk Mailers

As a way to utilize direct mail while keeping down mailing costs, many companies offer a variety of specialty card decks or coupon-type flyer assortments. Depending on the number of cards or flyers in a particular deck, your position in the pack itself and the target audience to which it is mailed, results will vary from almost non-existent to truly exceptional!

Another key element, obviously, is the appearance of your card or flyer and its appeal to your prospects. They have to notice your piece as worth pursuing even when it's mixed in with numerous competing ads.

Again, any mailing needs to clearly specify the BENEFITS you are offering to your prospects. Too many people confuse features with benefits and miss the mark in generating sufficient value for the prospect to create the interest needed to follow through and contact you.

Fax Lists

If your product line or business opportunity is appropriate for a particular professional or trade group, you can obtain a listing of facsimile numbers for that group and design a fax campaign. Such lists can often be purchased from companies specializing in that target market.

Design a single page, hard-hitting letter or ad, and fax it to those on your list. Although people are accustomed to tossing "junk mail" without even opening it, almost everyone reads their faxes! Follow up your fax with a phone call to gauge your prospect's interest.

Better yet, call to get permission to fax your offer before doing so. This will have a greater likelihood of being well-received. By alerting your prospect to expect your fax, you can develop rapport while exploring the other person's preferences. You can also get their commitment to read what you send – a very valuable commitment! – while letting them know that you will follow up to see if they care to learn more. You'll also avoid offending people by faxing without their permission.

Another technique to use if you don't have access to a fresh fax list, is to call a specific group from a phone list you have and request their fax numbers. If you are targeting a group of professionals likely to have fax machines (attorneys, realtors, doctors, etc.) simply tell the secretary or receptionist that you, "...would like to send Mr. Jones or Dr. Smith a fax, could you please have the fax number?" Fax your one-page letter or ad and then be prepared to follow it up with another phone call that same day or the very next day to check on the reaction to your information.

Flyers

Like direct mail and faxes, flyers can be one-page ads, letters, or promotional offers, but flyers can be put out in a number of different ways. They can also be professionally printed business cards/ads that can be widely circulated.

Your imagination is your only limitation as to where you distribute flyers. Possibilities include parking lots, airports, malls, or office buildings. Some networking distributors have successfully included flyers with newspaper deliveries or prominently displayed them on bulletin boards around town. Select areas which would likely have large numbers of prospects fitting your profile of an ideal distributor.

Caution: Make sure this type of advertising is appropriate to your target market! Flyers, even well-done ones, tend to be perceived as "cheap" by some people. Don't risk cheapening your image with advertising that's less than totally professional in the opinion of your target market.

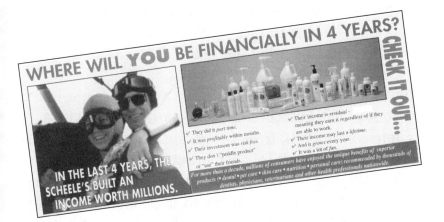

Examples of Flyers:

1. We Create Millionaires
*Success Magazine
To qualify you must
1. Have the capacity to lead others
2. Be willing to follow a simple, proven system
888-821-3135
Call for an interview.

2. Dream Income Potential
Help others lose weight
Guaranteed
Call for Free Wight Loss Sample and Free Report
800-999-9551 Ext. 970

3. If you're already making enough money,
GIVE THIS CARD TO A FRIEND,IF NOT,
CALL US AND WE'LL SEND YOU A CASSETTE TAPE
absolutely free describing the most exciting business
opportunity you've ever seen.
24-hour hot line 800 . . . .

Conventions and Trade Shows
Your product line or business opportunity may lend
itself to conventions, trade shows, business-to-business or
consumer fairs – events which bring large numbers of
high-quality prospects together in one location all at the
same time. Costs for renting booth space may range from a
few hundred to several thousand dollars. However, when

these costs are shared by several distributors, shows can be quite economical, as well as worthwhile.

It is of utmost importance for your booth to be professional, appealing, dynamic and welcoming. If you're a new vendor at a show or convention, you'd be well advised to attend a similar function as a customer first to get a precise idea of what others are doing and what would be most effective for you.

Bill and Taryn McKee of Yuba City, California, have built much of their large organization by scheduling monthly trade and professional shows. The McKee's suggest the following points to ensure your booth's success:

1. Never make product the only issue. If you are looking for business builders and entrepreneurs don't have product displays all over your booth. Your products are only the fuel that supports the opportunity. Don't let your prospects be confused about your purpose. It's not to sell products – it's to attract business partners. Talk about "Where will you be financially in 4 years?," "Exit the Rat Race," "Earn a Dream Income from Your Home," not about how good your skin care, toothpaste or widgets are.
2. Keep your booth open, don't block it off with a table in front and chairs which give people the excuse to keep on walking by. Stand and greet people, welcoming them to enter and explore the possibilities.
3. Keep your booth clean, inviting and professional in appearance. That means no greasy cheeseburgers, drinks or snacks!

4. Have periodic (hourly) business presentations available, given by your best speakers in a separate room. Cover the highlights of the network industry, your company, organization and opportunity, sharing a simple plan to show people how to succeed. Invite visitors to attend to explore the opportunity in more detail.

5. Have a guest register, enrollment form or prize drawing questionnaire to keep a record for later follow-up.

6. Remember to always smile, develop rapport and warmly encourage everyone to explore the possibilities without fear or obligation.

Bill DiPietro, another master at building via professional trade shows adds the following key pointers:

- Greet visitors warmly with an authentic demeanor.
- Show respect for their time by putting the important points of your presentation right up front.
- Decorate your booth with pictures that tell a story both about your most successful distributors and your products and their benefits.
- If possible, obtain a mailing list of show attendees and send out an attractive invitation encouraging them to visit your booth.

Not only can trade shows provide a great, accelerated learning experience for distributors to fine tune what may be missing from their presentations, but they allow for the ability to meet hundreds or even thousands of prospects face to face – thus paving the way for later deepening of the initial rapport and relationship established.

Business Presentation Meetings

Hosting opportunity or business presentation meetings can be an effective means of introducing large numbers of people to your opportunity. Meetings can be done in a variety of locations – ranging from distributors' homes to offices to hotel function rooms. The larger the gathering, the more detail-oriented the meeting needs to be. Everything from the lighting, room set up and the presence of slides, overheads or a white board, to the sequence of speakers, testimonials and meeting flow will affect the meeting's success. Meetings of this size will require competent, charismatic speakers to a greater degree than a smaller informal gathering. For this reason, smaller home meetings often are more duplicable and less labor and detail intensive.

Don and Mary Lou Vollmer of Denver, Colorado are masters at hosting and promoting the importance of local meetings. They have built an impressive million-dollar organization through a rigorous commitment to the weekly meeting format. Their weekly gatherings which take place both in their own home or at those of their leaders serve to provide a non-threatening introduction to new prospects, welcome new distributors to their duplicable system, and offer training on a wide range of business building topics.

The Vollmers cite the following elements as critical to the success of their meetings:

- The meetings are held at the same time and place every week to ensure that there is never any confusion as to where or when or even if a meeting will take place.
- The meetings generally last for approximately two hours – long enough to have an impact without becoming a dreaded burden.
- The size of the meeting is generally anywhere from a few people limited up to fifteen attendees tops. Once the meetings grow beyond these limits, up-and-coming leaders are encouraged to begin their own groupings. This not only ensures that proper personalized attention can be devoted to all but also champions new leaders to step into their own power as leaders themselves.
- At each meeting, a different person is responsible for preparing the agenda and actually conducting the event. The leader with the highest compensation plan position is responsible for the co-ordination of all topics and leaders.

Some of the agenda topics include:
- Sharing techniques for retailing.
- Creating structures and game plans for business building.
- Role-playing for prospecting, sorting and enrolling conversations.
- Discussions of key chapters of leading Network Marketing books such as those by Poe, Gage, Brooke and this book as well as a review and discussion of any appropriate network marketing training videos.

- Brainstorming sessions analyzing what's working and what's missing that if put into place would better enable distributors to succeed.
- Organization of group participation in co-operative ads, trade shows and other activities.

These weekly gatherings are an important element of the duplicable system that continually supports business building and new distributor participation. They serve to continually inspire, train and provide leadership at the local level. What's more, each group's weekly meetings serve as a nucleus funneling a consistent stream of new and empowered distributors into monthly opportunity and training meetings.

Cold Calling

Experienced telemarketers know that out of every 100 calls they make, only a few people will be interested in exploring the possibilities they have to offer. This volume-intensive technique is best employed by those who deal well with rejection. Knowing that there are people who want what you have to offer makes it worth sifting through all those who do not, but telemarketing is no place for the faint of heart – or fearful of purpose.

When cold calling, let your prospect know up front who you are, why you're calling, and how much time you are requesting from them. Find out if they'll spend three to five minutes exploring the possibilities with you. Develop a non-threatening approach that creates room for your prospect to check out what you are offering WITHOUT

OBLIGATION or RISK.

One way I like to create this kind of emotional space for people is by saying something like,

"Hi, my name is Joe Rubino, and I'm a dentist from Boston. I'm calling to ask if you would be willing to give me a little advice. It will take only about three minutes. Would that be all right?

"My company is expanding into the _____ market (veterinary, dental, nutrition, Southwest, chiropractic, New England, dermatology, etc.) and I'm looking for a person who might be interested in partnering with me to introduce our product line/business plan. The opportunity for the right person would be very rewarding (six figures annually). Would you or someone you know be interested in taking a look at our business plan with me?"

While cold calling can be effective when done by someone who communicates well and doesn't come across in a stilted, scripted way, it's a time-consuming technique that is successful only for those who don't mind hearing "No!" or a dial tone much of the time.

Mike Bonner of San Antonio, Texas, is the King of Cold Calls. Friendly and outgoing, with a wacky sense of humor, Mike has built his business largely by dropping in on several places of business every day for the last five years. Mike cites the key to his success as his willingness to talk about the awesome power of possibilities with anyone who will do so – without being attached to "getting them in" the business. In other words, the word "rejection" doesn't have any meaning for Mike. On any given day, Mike speaks with two groups of people, those willing to explore the possibilities and those who choose not to. To Mike, if there's a way his opportunity can contribute to his prospect, great! If not, he walks away enriched by yet another interesting conversation with another human being. Again, Mike is living proof that if you talk to enough people, some are bound to be interested.

Print Advertising

This is, by far, my favorite traditional way to prospect thousands of potential distributors who fit my ideal profile. There are two types of ads that can be placed in print: display ads and classified ads.

While display ads are more visible and allow for pictures, graphics, bold headings, testimonials, and colors, they can also be quite expensive.

Classified ads, though smaller and less flashy, are often the best value on the basis of how many calls you'll get for your money.

There are many publications in which your ad for prospects may be successful. Where you'll have the greatest response will depend on the type of program you are marketing, to whom it will most likely appeal, and the quality of the ad itself.

Let's go over a few possibilities of where to advertise.

1. Newspapers

Tailor your ad to fit your product line and opportunity. Classified ads are the least expensive and can be a great source of leads.

My favorite publication – because of the results I've gotten – is USA Today. A classified ad in the "Business Opportunity" section reaches a receptive audience throughout America.

The average reader earns more than $40,000 per year – the perfect target for a networking opportunity. USA Today is heavily circulated by hotels and airlines, and it's read by many business-minded people.

Also, although there are only about 200,000 regular subscribers, the circulation exceeds one million Monday through Thursday, and it jumps to two million on Friday! As a result, different people are constantly being exposed to your ad, which should continue to draw well for an extended period.

So far, not that many individuals are aware of the benefits USA Today offers, so, as a result, there are relatively few ads run on a daily basis. This makes your ad more visible and less likely to get lost in the crowd.

Another place for classified ads can be your local and regional suburban newspapers. Ads focused on particular products and those who use them are particularly appropriate for this market. Pick up a copy of the newspaper you're considering, and check out all the other ads being run. Look for those ads that are repeated regularly. You may need to market-test a few different ads with different headlines and offer "hooks" before finding the one that works best for you.

Other national publications that have circulation's of several million, such as the National Inquirer or the Star, can be cost-effective ways to reach specific demographics – typically women over age 35. If your company's profile and products fit this market, these leads may be your best value.

2. National and Regional Magazines

Like newspaper advertising, classified ads in these magazines reach large numbers of people nationwide for a reasonable cost. *Home Business, Working Woman, Entrepreneur, Boston Magazine, Selling, Nation's Business, Inc., Income Opportunities* and any of the airline magazines are a few proven examples.

The value of these ads on a cost-per-quality-lead basis is usually high.

It's important here to stress the need to differentiate your offer from all the competition. Make your ad unique and compelling with benefits. Design it to stimulate interest and arouse curiosity, and have people take action by calling you immediately.

3. Industry-Specific Magazines and Journals

If your company markets a heavy-duty cleaner that mechanics, janitors, or cleaning services might use, look for publications that people in these groups subscribe to because of their work. Depending on your budget, either classified or display ads might be best for you.

You can write your ad to concentrate on your products or on your opportunity. To determine which focus to take, decide if you want to attract product users or people interested in an income opportunity.

If your focus is on product, you are likely to attract buyers. It's true that a percentage of these leads can be persuaded to look at your business plan, but that is not what caught their attention in the first place.

If you really want to attract entrepreneurs, advertise your opportunity rather than product.

4. Newsletters

Many groups, industries, or professions publish local or national newsletters for their members. Classified or display ads in these publications target a very particular market.

Put yourself in the reader's shoes to discover issues of interest or discontent common to that demographic group. For example, if you want to approach workers in an industry plagued by layoffs – which is, today, the single biggest fear of American workers – write your ad to address their discontent and insecurity about the future. Try something like, "Has downsizing cast a cloud over your future...?" If your market is small businesses harassed by OSHA, use that situation to your advantage with a, "Are government regulations taking the creativity and freedom out of your job...?" approach.

5. MLM Publications

Such publications as *Money Makers' Monthly, Income Opportunities, Profit and Opportunity, Cutting Edge*, and others are published specifically for network marketers. The advantage of these publications is an already MLM-receptive audience. The downside is increased competition with other distributors and opportunities. Also, MLM "junkies" tend to frequent these sources more often than people looking for just one business opportunity.

If you do advertise in MLM publications, look to distinguish what you have to offer from everyone else's approach. Appeal to a particular group or profession. Stress such benefits as longevity, new product introductions, sizzle products, foreign expansion, exploding company growth, success of current distributors, or national awards or recognitions.

Experienced MLMers look for such elements as a renewable superior product line, a well-capitalized, debt-free company with an established support structure, and company leadership with expertise and integrity – elements that address their dissatisfaction with their current opportunity.

Free Publicity Through Press Releases

Another means in which to spread the word about your networking business is through press releases. Not only is a story about what you do printed in a newspaper or magazine or told on television or radio a tremendous way to enhance your credibility in the community – but you can't beat the cost. That is, it's free!

An effective press release can focus on how you support people to create successful home-based businesses or it can focus on a unique aspect of your products, company or opportunity. The key to getting a press release noticed is that it must be of widespread human interest or relate some unique and noteworthy story that can be of contribution to others.

Newspaper and magazine editors are a particularly good place to begin in your search for free publicity. They have an obligation to both come up with stories that are of interest to others as well as to fill out any remaining space in each issue of their paper or magazine before it can go to print.

So, first identify how your story is appealing and newsworthy. Next, identify the appropriate editor or writer to contact at the newspaper or magazine. It is often easier to obtain publicity in a local town or community publication than in a big city or national journal.

Look for similar articles in the publications you have

an interest in contacting and notice who the writers are. Or go to your local library and look for "Bacon's Newspaper Directory" in the reference section. Look up the newspaper in question and the name of the corresponding editor for the topic of your release.

Once you've targeted the appropriate journals, call first to share your story and follow up with your release, fact sheet, photo and any other pertinent information. Ask the paper's receptionist when the best time to reach the journalist is, so as not to call at an inconvenient time. Most papers' deadlines are in the early afternoon so try calling around mid-morning.

Introduce yourself, ask if it's a good time to call or when the writer may be free. If it's a good time, share the highlights of your story and ask if the writer might entertain reviewing it. Speak from the heart and seek to develop rapport first. Share your story in a newsy and exciting way, pointing out any areas of controversy that might further add to the story's appeal.

If the writer shows some interest, send your story immediately, either overnight or priority mail and mark your package "Requested Information." From time to time, follow up to see if your information was received and if any further details are requested.

The same technique would apply regarding television and radio stations. If your story is unique enough or stimulates sufficient interest, you may find yourself being interviewed on the radio or with a television crew showing up to do a brief human interest story airing on the 6 o'clock news.

Lastly, if writing is one of your talents, you might submit an article for review by either a network marketing journal or professional or trade magazine linked to your topic. Include a short paragraph about yourself, how you might contribute to its readers and a toll-free number to reach you.

With a little creativity and effort you can reach a large audience at no, or little, expense while enhancing your image and creating credibility in the community at the same time.

Television and Radio Commercials

Both of these media have been sparsely utilized by network marketers. Radio spots can be quite cost-effective in getting your company name recognized and in generating real interest from prospects.

The challenge to prospects with radio is inconvenience. If they must stop whatever they're doing – like driving to or from work – to write down your phone number they're less likely to make the call.

Certain "sizzle" products can fare better on radio, especially when the ads are repeated with enough frequency to generate productive response.

Many companies are also experiencing success with radio infomercials of about 30 minutes in length. Such info-commercials resemble the format of a radio talk show while providing frequent mention of an 800 number to call for more information. If professionally produced and run on talk stations frequented by an audience receptive to your offering, these infomercials can be quite productive. And the cost to produce and air these ads can be shared among several people to make them more affordable.

Television or cable commercials (usually 30 to 120 seconds long) are not yet in wide use by MLMers. The several-thousand-dollar price tag on quality production of even a short commercial, followed by the air time costs, is prohibitive for most distributors. But again, these expenses can be shared in an ad campaign among several distributors.

When you factor in the difficulty of condensing your entire message to a minute or less, the project becomes even more challenging. However, these commercials do reach large audiences quickly. The important question to ask yourself is not "Will it work?" Ask instead, "Will my distributors be able to do the same thing with these commercials to build their businesses?"

One way to keep the air time costs down to a manageable level is to contract to have your radio or TV commercial, or infomercial, aired on a "backup" only basis. If the regularly-priced slots have not all been sold, many radio and TV stations offer this standby availability to insure against "dead air" and unprofitable down time.

If you take advantage of this arrangement, it's possible that your ad will air for up to 90 percent less than guaranteed time rates, making this form of electronic advertising much more cost effective.

Television Infomercials

When done correctly, no other Direct Response paid advertising medium can yield the volume of customers and brand awareness as fast, and, as cost effectively as TV infomercials. However, producing and airing a successful infomercial is not without risk. It is estimated that only one out of ten infomercials makes a profit. Another factor that acts as a deterrent for testing infomercials is cost. Just the production costs alone for successful infomercials can range anywhere from $75,000 to as much as $ 1,500,000 for those involving top name celebrities. If someone has a large enough budget, this method of advertising can cause stellar returns – although few can duplicate it, much less afford it.

So why the allure? Why would an MLM company or distributor even consider testing an infomercial when the stakes are so high?

The answer is simple. No other paid advertising medium can provide the return on investment as fast as a successful infomercial. In addition, only infomercials can generate such a vast source of new customers and distributors for MLM organizations and provide a long stream of profits starting right after the initial advertising investment is recovered.

Perhaps, one of the greatest benefits that infomercials can provide is a new source of MLM prospects who do not necessarily have a pre-conceived negative bias toward network marketing. Because infomercial customers are typically sold on the product first by a convincing TV infomercial, they tend to be open to learning how they can receive the product for FREE and even make money by recommending it to others.

According to Mitch Wiggenhorn of Phillips DRTV Group, a company that specializes in producing and integrating infomercials with network marketing, the odds of having a successful infomercial campaign that returns a profit are dramatically increased by following what Wiggenhorn calls the "Six Cardinal Rules" of producing and testing an infomercial.

They are:

Rule #1 The product advertised must have a minimum of a 5 to 1 mark-up. In other words the cost to produce the product must be no greater than 20% of what the consumer pays for it. Therefore, if you are selling a month's supply of product for $49.95, you better not be paying more than $10.00 for the month's supply.

Rule #2 Never self-produce your own infomercial, unless you have recently produced a successful one in the same product category. Most failures occur because novices believe that they can produce an infomercial for their product that is as good, or even better, than those they see on TV. Approximately 66% of all failed infomercials are produced by someone that had not previously produced an infomercial in the same product category. If successful infomercials were easy to do, there would not be a 90% failure rate! There are a countless number of factors that go into producing a successful infomercial. Unless you have unlimited funds and two to three years to test all the different variables that go into a successful production, you should use a producer that has already "paid the price." A good producer usually has better than a 50% success factor.

Rule #3 Think twice before selecting a product category that has not had considerable success with other top rated infomercials. Exercise equipment, diet, home business opportunities, vanity products (skin care, cosmetics, skin blemish remedies, hair care, etc.), automobile care, kitchen appliances, golf/fishing and self-improvement/ relationships are all categories that have had many successes. About three out of nine failures occur because "entrepreneurs" think that their product will beat the odds and be the first one on TV to reap the benefits. Unfortunately, the vast majority of infomercials based upon brand new "widgets" that do not fall within one of the eight categories listed above have usually failed. Remember, TV viewers are not innovators. They are typically followers who simply want a "better mouse trap." With the exception of the golf/fishing category, which appeals to a very zealous niche market, all the other categories appeal to a very broad market.

Rule #4 Unless you are planning a short-term infomercial campaign to "knock-off" a competitive "look-alike" product, your product must have its own Unique Selling Proposition (USP) in order to have a winning long-term program. TV consumers will only buy your product if it appears better than your competitor's or if it seems easier or more effective to use. Many infomercials fail because the product too closely resembles something consumers have already bought – or something that they have already seen on TV and made the decision not to buy.

Rule #5 The product must be proven. It must either have extensive research behind it, or many convincing case studies and testimonials supporting its effectiveness...or preferably, both of these. Many infomercials fail because the entrepreneur is too anxious to advertise his product before enough convincing evidence has been collected. The exception to this rule is when the infomercial uses a well-known celebrity or authority figure to endorse and recommend the product. The latter method usually ends up costing the marketer much more and returning less of a profit.

Rule #6 The product must be consumable and have a high reorder rate. The only way MLM distributors will support an infomercial campaign is if they can recoup their initial advertising investment and have an ongoing revenue stream. Since the revenue generated from consumers' initial orders are typically only enough to pay-back the advertising investment and cover product and overhead costs, the products that fare best are renewable consumables. Products like exercise equipment, golf/fishing, relationship tapes, etc. will typically not work for network marketing unless there is a consumable product that accompanies the initial purchase.

If you're still thinking, "Why should I consider such an expensive option for building my MLM business?" There are other reasons that integrating an infomercial with network marketing may be a sound business decision.

The cost to produce an infomercial for a network marketing Company or distributor organization is substantially less than it is for companies outside of the MLM industry because the infomercial can be shot with much less administrative production effort and in much less time. The reason for this is that it is much easier to find the testimonials and experts that will be videotaped for the infomercial from the ranks of the distributor force. Also, most of the best testimonial and expert candidates tend to work their MLM business in distinct geographic areas which can cut down tremendously on travel time and related costs.

Moreover, no one gives better "heartfelt" testimonials than network marketers. Because they believe so strongly in their products, their testimonials are believable and therefore convince TV viewers that they really need to try the product. Having believable testimonials is the most critical creative factor necessary for having a successful infomercial.

Even if the infomercial does not generate the desired up-front revenue from TV, versions of it can be used for recruiting and sales-aid tapes. There have been many incidents whereby the revenue generated from tape sales alone have been more than sufficient to recoup the initial advertising investment and return a nice profit! Again, networkers have a distinct advantage over marketers outside of network marketing by being able to leverage their up-front risk by creating another profitable revenue stream.

Lastly, there are many Local Cable Origination TV stations (LCOs) that will air infomercials at extremely low advertising rates. Typically, the infomercial could air up to 10 to 14 times during a two week period for as little as

$250 to $1000. These airings are ideal to stimulate local interest and generate attendance at a local organization's opportunity and business building meetings. This is yet another distinct advantage that networkers have by being able to use the infomercial for other business building purposes.

According to Wiggenhorn of *Phillips DRTV Group*, if you are an MLM company or distributor with a sizeable organization and have the ability to raise between $75,000 to $100,000 to produce and test an infomercial, you would have better than an 80% chance of launching a successful infomercial by partnering with his company. Over the last ten years *Phillips DRTV Group* has tested 11 different MLM infomercials of which 9 have proven extremely successful. These 9 infomercials have generated over $200,000,000 in revenue and over 1,250,000 customers of which approximately 15% have become network marketing distributors. In addition, because *Phillips DRTV Group* has had so much success, they often choose to participate in helping to finance an infomercial campaign if they like the product and can put together a pro-forma that will work.

Although they turn down the majority of products and opportunities submitted to them, Wiggenhorn and his partner, Tina Phillips (602- 596-3944) offer a free information kit to allow interested parties to determine if their product might be right for an infomercial home run.

Prospecting Online

As network marketing evolves into the 21st century, the marvels of the information age are becoming the everyday tools of our trade. The technological advances of the 90's consisting of fax machines, three-way calling, voice mail, conference calling and dial-up modems have evolved into high speed Internet connections, video streaming, online video chat rooms, Internet phone service, auto-responders, online downline-building systems and a variety of other technologically advanced tools to facilitate building a network marketing downline with velocity. The expansion of cyberspace has provided an arena in which we can now literally prospect staggering numbers – up to millions of online opportunity-seekers on a daily or weekly basis.

Millions of people across the globe communicate via the Internet daily. The Strategis Group, a Washington-based market research firm, noted than more than half of all American adults now use the Internet. In the USA alone, this means that there are currently more than 130 million people connected to the Internet with conservative estimates of at least 200 million within the next few years. Not only are more people going online, but more and more Internet users are becoming more sophisticated in their use of the Internet as a tool for communication, commerce and education. The average user sends more than ten emails a day. The number of home business websites is growing at the rate of twenty percent per quarter. Access Markets International reports that the 28.8 million Internet-connected small businesses spent $78.8 billion dollars globally in 2002 on over 12 million web sites. Over 13 million small businesses have deployed high-speed Internet connections, spending nearly $17 billion — almost twice that spent in 2002 on dial-up access.

As more and more people conduct business online, the potential for network marketing organizational growth through the use of this medium increases exponentially. The Web presents the opportunity to showcase anything from commercial advertising for products or services to descriptions of companies and business opportunities. With the touch of a button, you can receive or share information on any topic imaginable. There are literally tens of thousands of sites where you can place free ads for business opportunities, for sale of products or services, or for anything else you might want to promote. There are also countless sites that allow for advertising your company, products or opportunity in exchange for a fee.

There is also an endless and ever-expanding pool of people online who are looking to develop their own home-based businesses by tapping into the information and prospects available online. Prospecting in the computer world has many obvious advantages. You can reach millions of people daily, people who are specifically looking for business opportunities or products you have to offer. Responses via email are either fully automated or quickly typed on a keyboard and received instantly. Although there is a monthly use-charge for accessing Internet service -- in the $10-$25 range for a dial-up connection to $50 or more for high-speed cable or DSL access – email is free. You can obtain an email address through your Internet service provider or from any of the free services such as Yahoo, Mail.com, Hotmail or several others.

One nice thing about using cyberspace to prospect is the cost. Classified ads on computer bulletin boards are often free or quite inexpensive compared to newspaper advertising. There are literally thousands of free classified ad sites and topic-specific news groups from which to choose. The low cost, in relation to the potential audience you can reach, is one of the main attractions of prospecting online. However, be fore-warned. Be prepared to get reverse prospected anytime you advertise on sites available for all to see. The shear numbers of MLM distributors using these free sites to advertise has created a free-for-all atmosphere with much competition. Because of this, there are other more effective ways to attract people online. If you do decide to advertise online, it is advisable to get a "throw-away" email address at any of the free email sites like Yahoo, Hotmail, Gobot, Mail.com, or others. You can use this email address in your ads and even track your advertising effectiveness by using several different email addresses. Doing so will allow you to relegate to these disposable email addresses the amount of SPAM (unsolicited email) you will certainly attract by exposing your email address on public sites. This will allow you to keep your primary email address relatively spam-free.

Today, most leading MLM companies offer their distributors the opportunity to purchase a duplicable, personalized website that promotes the company's products and opportunity. Such a personalized site, often equipped with sound and an enrolling video flash presentation, contains a special URL or website address that identifies the distributor-owner and allows for accurate tracking of all prospects visiting the site and all customer orders placed. In addition to the duplicable aspect of providing a professional looking company website, another benefit is that it eliminates the need for individual distributors to have their own personal websites promoting the company, products or opportunity. This removes any possibility that independent distributors may make dangerous online product or income claims that might attract regulators' scrutiny and bring damaging legal repercussions.

If there is any downside to computer prospecting, it's the fact that ads do attract many lookers without necessarily producing qualified leads. The more high-tech our industry becomes, the most important it is that we maintain the element of high-touch relationship building. To develop the all-important bonding with prospects and potential future business partners, it is critical to follow-up and qualify your prospect's interest and motivation. Although you may have attracted your prospect via the Internet, it still makes sense to offer a phone conversation to answer questions, get to know what is important to your new potential partner and support his or her success by formulating a sound business plan.

Prospecting With Opt-In Email

One alternative to the unacceptable practice of spamming (sending bulk, unsolicited email messages) is through the use of opt-in email. Several online companies offer the ability to mail to their targeted lists of online prospects who have actually agreed to receiving information on a certain subject. Opt-in lists cover a wide range of topics including home based business and MLM opportunity seekers, weight loss prospects, those interested in health and nutrition as well as numerous other interests. Costs to mail to such lists typically range from a low of about $.03 to as much as $.25 or more per name purchased. While some opt-in companies offer a one-time mailing that is transmitted for you, others sell you the list of names and email addresses for your repeated use. In addition, some companies provide free use of auto-responder systems which can be programmed with multiple and varied advertisements or other messages scheduled to email to your list at whatever desired intervals you program into the system. Such a system can serve as an effective way to automatically drip on your prospects for any time period up to a year or longer, if desired. What distinguishes a successful mailing from one with poor response has to do with both the quality of the list mailed to and the attractiveness of the offer. The more specific the offer is that the prospect responded to, the higher the quality the lead would be. Opt-in lists are, by definition, higher quality than opt-out lists in which participants may not really be interested in what is offered but never bother to remove themselves from the list. Lists compiled through deceptive means or covertly through less understandable co-registration practices will often be of little value. Usually, the better qualified the prospect, the more costly the list. Only testing of a list will determine if it is more cost effective to mail to 100,000 leads costing $.07 each or to 1000 leads costing $7.00 each.

Beware of companies that sell names and email addresses that were harvested from newsgroups, chatrooms and other online sources without the knowledge or permission of the so-called prospects. Such lists are actually not prospect lead lists at all but cold lists of unsolicited names. Sending your offer to such lists without the recipients' permission will result in accusations of spamming. This will not only damage your reputation and label you as an unethical marketer but will likely cause your Internet service provider or domain name registration company to terminate your service and report you to the authorities.

Banner Ads

Another way to attract customers and prospects online is through the use of banner and button ads. Web sites that generate a great deal of traffic often offer banner rentals that attract prospects to your offer. Your banner, prominently displayed on a busy website or as part of an online ezine or newsletter, can be effective in enticing interested parties to click on your benefit-driven offer to learn more. Advertising costs are usually determined either by the number of impressions (times that your banner ad is displayed to visitors to the site) or actual click-throughs (times that a visitor clicks on your banner to learn more about your offer) or even by the number of actual leads gathered. The more qualified the lead, the more effective the advertising campaign will be.

In addition to the option of purchasing banner ads, there are also several banner-exchange programs that will trade displaying your banner on their member sites in exchange for you displaying their banners on your website. If your own website generates a good amount of traffic and the banners offered through the exchange program do not conflict with your own offer, banner exchanges can be an effective way to generate additional free leads.

Online Malls

Many companies offer virtual store space in any of numerous online malls, which are usually organized around a particular theme. For example, there are malls designed around health products, crafts, moneymaking opportunities, MLM, mail order and many other topics. The idea is that the mall owner advertises to bring interested online shoppers to the mall. This, in turn, stimulates interest in your virtual store, which rents space from the mall owner. While some web malls are successful in generating traffic, most are not. Just because you are part of a mall does not guarantee that you will be overrun with traffic, interest or sales. Be sure to ask for references and statistics from other tenants before committing to virtual office space.

Website Traffic Generators

There are thousands of different traffic generators being offered to increase traffic to your website. Some of these include the following ways to attract others to your site: classified ad capability (offering free classified ads), postcard or greeting card generators (offering a range of free online postcards or special occasion cards), reminder systems (people program in important dates like birthdays, anniversaries, etc.), list-generators (people are added to specific theme lists offering jokes, horoscopes, inspirational sayings, poetry, business or factual information as well as countless other topics), as well as many other types of traffic generators. The idea behind these traffic stimulators is that you can place a banner ad prominently displayed on the page offering the free service. As you attract visitors to your free enticement, they see your banner, click on it, and are exposed to your offer. While the concept sounds feasible in theory, its effectiveness will be totally dependent on the aggressiveness in advertising to bring visitors to your site. Without a constant source of ads promoting these devises both online or in traditional advertising, few prospects will ever find them. What's more, be sure to thoroughly research the various companies offering such services, which can be quite costly. Often times, similar services or products may be available at little or no cost from other sources.

Email Traffic Generators

Another type of traffic generator involves the so-called "safe-list." In this type of advertising, companies typically sell the unsuspecting traffic-seeker the offer of sending their classified ad, display ad or advertisement letter to a large number of people who are supposedly on a safe-list, meaning they have agreed to receive such offers. The way this program usually works is the advertiser also agrees to receive other offers in return. Everyone in such a program is advised to get a disposable free email address to be used exclusively for this purpose. As a result, your "junk-mail" box gets filled with thousands of offers and your advertisement is likewise sent to thousands of others who, like you, seldom, if ever, check these junk-mail messages.

Pop-Up or Pop-Under Banner Ads

This form of advertising promises a large number of actual website visits to those who participate. A mirror page resembling your actual website or a smaller banner leading visitors to your site pops up over or under another website you have chosen to visit. Although this form of advertising can be effective if your banner or site is very compelling, most people will automatically delete these intrusive and what many consider to be annoying banners when they appear over or behind the site being visited. Many will even set their computer settings to disable such banners. Again, it would be prudent to request references before spending money on this sort of advertising medium.

Generic Lead Generation Companies

In lieu of taking on the need to advertise on your own, a number of lead generation companies offer a service whereby they do the advertising for you. They place advertisements either online or in traditional publications such as newspapers, magazines and card decks, with the intention of attracting prospects with a generic work-at-home type offer. These companies then offer these leads to distributors in multiple companies for various costs ranging a few cents each to up to $10 or more. Some are very poor quality, having been gathered covertly or with questionable techniques. For example, some forms of co-registration deceive registrants into opting-in for offers with the promise of some reward or prize for doing so. Co-registration involves when an online prospect or customer purchases a product or fills out personal information on some offer and after doing so agrees to receive additional offers on any of several topics selected. Unfortunately, sometimes co-registration is done via the fine print in an agreement resulting in "prospects" not recalling having agreed to receive offers. Also, less effective is an opt-out process whereby suspects are considered prospects until they opt-out and decline further offers. Other times, co-registration and lead gathering is done in a clear and effective manner resulting in higher quality leads.

Some companies also offer various degrees of pre-qualifying prospects. They may require one or two forms to be filled out by the prospect detailing his or her personal information and interests. Some companies even call the prospects to verify that they are still interested in receiving offers and to gage their seriousness as someone who is genuinely interested in receiving offers. Obviously, the more qualified the prospect, the more expensive the lead cost will be. Always, remember, it is not so much the cost per lead that is the critical factor but the overall resulting cost per distributor obtained. For some network marketing offers, the more expensive leads will be a better investment. With others, it may be more cost effective to purchase more leads at a lower per lead cost. The latter approach relies on success through numbers. The best strategy is to purchase a test batch of leads and follow them up aggressively, tracking your response statistics and the final resulting cost per new distributor.

Pay-per-click Lead Generation

Many search engine sites, Internet portals and other high traffic websites offer a pay-per-click lead generation model whereby advertisers typically pay between $.01 and $1.00 each time their offers are clicked upon by visitors to the advertising website. This type of lead generation can prove to be quite cost-effective and many sites offer low cost trial programs ranging from $20 to $50 or more to test an offer's effectiveness.

Some websites take this concept a step further and charge only for prospects that actually enter their name, email address and other information into a survey form designed to gather lead information. These pay-per-lead sites often charge in to the $2.00 to $5.00 per lead range although some charge considerably more. Like any other means of lead generation, it is prudent to test the cost-effectiveness of such a model with a small test-buy before deciding to follow-up with a more significant investment.

Newsletters and Ezines

There are many thousand newsletters being produced and distributed daily on every topic under the sun. One viable way to attract prospects to your products or opportunity is to develop an informational online publication that is of value, offering it at no cost to anyone willing to accept a subscription. As you invite people interested in the topic of your newsletter to accept a free subscription, you add their names to a list-server, which, with a few key-strokes, allows you to send your publication easily and for free to everyone on the list. As your circulation grows, you can add a classified ad section to your newsletter offering your products or opportunity as well as those of others who either purchase ad space from you or swap ads with you in a reciprocal arrangement. This can be an effective manner of promoting an offer provided that your subscription list grows to a significant size and offers true value in content.

Of course, you can also seek out those ezines or online newsletters that mail to your target audience. Many offer inexpensive and effective classified ads that can be cooped with members of your organization.

Online Downline Builders

One of the most exciting advances in building a network marketing organization online has been brought about by combining the vast reach of the Internet with the ability to send mass mailings to lists of opt-in opportunity seekers and build a downline automatically with those who respond to an offer and tour your website. Such systems not only gather prospects' information as they tour your site but have automated follow-up email systems in place to educate, excite and inspire prospects to take action. The best systems act as a perfect sponsor would. These contain automatically generated messages that create rich possibilities for prospects by demonstrating the simplicity of building with such a system. They further contain messages and links that provide written, audio or video training, incentive messages rewarding prospects to take action and messages that remind them of impending events and profitable opportunities for action.

Several companies offer their own branded version of a downline builder site. Some of the most rapidly growing systems even offer their distributors the option of purchasing a guaranteed number of registered members who have toured the distributor's website. These "trial members" are much more qualified than typical networking leads as each has not only toured the company's offer but entered their name, email address, phone number, income level desired and other helpful information in order to gain access to the site.

Generic downline builder services are also available. You can generate a list of companies that offer these services by putting the words such as downline builder, mlm recruiting system, network marketing lead generation or MLM duplicator in any search engine such as Google.com or Yahoo.com.

Combining Online With Traditional Advertising and Prospecting

For me, this approach works best.

A well designed website that is promoted on business cards, stationery, in traditional and online ads and in other ways offers an effective way to show the world what you have to offer. Such a site can greatly reduce the need to send out expensive sorting packages while eliminating the delay of snail mail. While not all of your prospects will be online, most will and these people can gain access to your benefits in the time it takes to type in your website address. When you combine the efficiency the Internet offers with the effectiveness of personal communication, rapport and relationship building, you can truly have the best of both worlds.

Prospecting online is certainly a source full of possibilities for rapid growth of your business. I know of no other cost-effective medium that can put your message in front of so many people so quickly. This technology, coupled with all the other techniques for developing qualified leads, can provide the ultimate foundation for anyone's success in network marketing.

No matter which combination of these or other sources for prospects you may utilize, the important point is to ensure that you consistently have more names than you can handle!

When your supply of prospects is never-ending, each one can be approached powerfully and without any sense of urgency or desperation. The old saying, "Some will. Some won't. So what. Next!" rings true only if there are hundreds more "next" new potential partners waiting in the wings.

Create a Game Plan and Track Your Results

You will not know which niche and method of prospecting will provide you with the greatest success until you track your results. Commit to prospecting 100 individuals in each of three to five different niche markets. Perhaps these niches might include your profession, church group, school class, children's soccer team's parents, and your club list. Decide how many hours per week you can devote to your prospecting efforts. Commit to a *single daily action* that consists of a minimum number of daily conversations you will make day in and day out in each of your niche groups. Be creative in obtaining your prospect leads. Perhaps many will come from your warm market, consisting of people you know. Others may come from ads targeting the specific type of prospect you are seeking. Advertise for chiropractors in a chiropractic journal and for Spanish speaking individuals in a Hispanic newspaper, etc. Prospect for men with ads in men's magazines. Ask those in positions of credibility and authority with the group you seek to suggest ways to target them.

Buy a spiral-bound notebook or create a computer file and record the following statistics in it on a daily basis:

- Date of the conversation
- Name, address, phone, fax, email address, etc. of the prospect
- How you obtained the lead (which ad, referral, warm market contact, etc.)
- Important facts about the prospect including family, occupation, where she lives, hobbies, areas of interest, concerns and challenges

Answer the following questions to gage your progress:
- Did you develop rapport and get to know your prospect sufficiently?
- Did you create an opening to be heard and appreciated?
- Did you identify what was important or missing in his life?
- Did you create value and rich possibilities?
- Did your prospect get that you are successful and that you have a commitment to support her to be successful?
- What worked?

- What was missing, that if put into place, would make the next prospecting conversation more effective?

Do this for at least 500 prospecting conversations in any number of niche markets while tracking your results as you go and you will be well on your way to achieving network marketing success.

The consistency that comes with the habit of speaking to scores of new people will eventually insure your success. Being consistently consistent, means developing work habits that support your goals. Broken down to the least common denominator, this looks like a daily action that, when repeated religiously, will guarantee your success. Even the best prospecting lead is worthless if not pursued promptly and powerfully! Here's how it's done.

Your Single Daily Actions

Good organization is essential to success in any endeavor. This is especially true for new network marketing distributors. Let's take a look at what you will need to organize on a daily basis to guarantee your success.

1. Prospecting

Getting back to the concept of success ratios, how many people would you need to prospect on a daily basis to be on track to achieve your goals for a given month? (Remember, in our earlier example, we decided you would need to have, on average, 200 prospecting conversations to identify one leader.)

If your goal was to find one future leader this month, and you worked Monday through Friday, or 20 days in the month, you would need to prospect 10 people each day to stay on track. Your single daily action here would include 10 prospecting conversations each and every working day. To ground your goal in your ability to do the actions needed to accomplish the result, you would need to either commit the time and effort required to carry out these 10 conversations daily OR expand your time limit for reaching your goal. You would also need to know sources for 200 names. This is the first step in grounding your actions in realistic relationship to your goals.

As I said before, the number of people you would need to prospect to identify one leader varies greatly from person to person. Developing your communication skills and effectiveness will lower the number of prospecting conversations you need to have to obtain the same result.

Later on in the book, we'll look at why it is that one person may need to have 200 conversations to identify one leader, while another may need to have only half as many conversations to get those very same results.

2. Sorting

I define a "sorting" conversation as a quality conversation that is the next step and the natural result of successful prospecting.

Sorting includes the process of trying the products and reviewing materials to determine if a prospect is interested in becoming a retail customer, a wholesale customer, and/or taking a look at the business opportunity to see if it fits their "why."

We'll do more about sorting later, as well. For now, let's determine how many sorting conversations you will need to have daily to be on track for your monthly goal.
Based on your historical overall ratios, let's say you determine that you need four sorting conversations each day to reach your goals – your single daily actions would need to include those as well.

3. Follow-up Conversations

After you've had a quality sorting conversation to explore the possibilities of your products or business opportunity, your prospects will most likely need to try products, watch a video, listen to an audio tape, or read some literature on your company, products, or opportunity. Each of those activities will take time, so you will have to follow up with a third conversation.

You'll need to calculate how many of these follow-up conversations you need to keep the flow going with your prospects as they explore what you're offering. Include the required number of follow-up conversations in your single daily actions, too.

4. Miscellaneous Activity

This category includes all other actions which occur daily as needed to ensure your success.

Included here are the number of sorting packages you will need to send out to prospects, the training or coaching you'll take part in with your upline and downline, reading of company literature or books on network marketing, watching video tapes, bookkeeping, listening to audio tapes, conference calls, etc. In other words, anything else that would support your business-building activities. Set aside a specific number of hours each day for these activities and include them in your single daily actions.

So, ...

Given that you need to prospect 200 people to identify one leader and you prospect 20 days per month:

If you:	You will:
Prospect 10 per day	Identify 1 leader per month.
Prospect 5 per day	Identify one leader in 2 months.
Prospect 1 per day	Identify 1 leader in 10 months.

Your Single Daily Actions will include:

- Prospect X people per day
- Send out X sorting packages per day
- Follow up with X prospects per day
- X time for miscellaneous activities per day

Up to this point, we've covered half of the equation for success in prospecting. That is, the numbers game. Now, let's look at the equally-important flip side of the coin of prospecting success.

Chapter Four

How Attractive are YOU as a Potential Business Partner?

You know your source for names.

You've identified a number of strategies for presenting your company, products and opportunity.

You've calculated just how many presentations and calls you need to make.

So, the question is, how will you make the most of these conversations?

One way is to develop yourself as a powerful, attractive, prospective sponsor and business partner.

Check Your State of Mind and Maintain Your Posture

When you contact a new prospect, do you ask yourself, "Who am I being that would either attract or turn off this prospect?"

Are you organized, calm, and focused – or are you nervous, rushed, and flustered?

Is your presentation enthusiastic and powerful – or weak and whiny?

Does your prospect sense any urgency or desperation in your voice? Have you conveyed to them that you would love to work with them in building a business – but you do not NEED them to join you?

Do you project success and confidence?

Have you checked your belief level?

Do you have any unresolved objections about what you are doing?

Do you understand the powerful network marketing concepts well enough to share your belief in them with others?

What is your interpretation of sharing your opportunity with your prospect – i.e. are you intruding and bothering them or offering them the gift of the awesome power of possibilities?

Closely examine your presentation. If you're prospecting in person, does your dress and appearance speak of success? Do you value your time and your prospects' and convey this to them, or do you seem to have all the time in the world, implying that you're really not up to much?

When you speak, use the combined credibility of your company and its most successful leaders. Be proud of what you do. Convey your certainty that it is a privilege to work with you and your company.

Got the idea?

So, what I'm really asking is,

"Would you want you as a business partner...?"

To answer, first check out your belief level.

How Strong Is Your Belief?

There was once an uneducated immigrant who had come to America. He was illiterate and hard of hearing – but he made great hot dogs. He would stand by the side of the road with his cart and sell his hot dogs. He did very well.

One day, his son – he'd earned enough money to send the young man away to school – came home from college and said to his father, "Don't you know how bad the economy is? Everyone is starving, being laid off, going bankrupt."

The old man thought, "My son must know. He can read and write. He's gone to college." So he took down his sign. He cut back on his meat and bun orders, and he stopped going out beside the road.

Guess what happened?

His business declined and kept declining until he could no longer support himself. Finally, he was forced to close down.

And the old man said, "My son was right. The economy is so bad, no one could make it in times like these."

As you build your networking business, your level of belief is critical to your success. Whether you consciously realize it or not, the people you speak to about joining you in business are certain to pick up on whether you really believe you will succeed.

It's in the energy you project. It's who you are. You are either someone who radiates success – or you do not.

If your expectations of success are strong, they will generate the motivation you need to act, to do whatever it takes to succeed.

If, on the other hand, you don't really expect to succeed, your actions will reflect that as you subconsciously sabotage yourself, take down your sign and stop offering your hot dogs.

Belief in your ultimate success is critical. If you don't really have it, associate with those who do. Take on a mentor who can coach you to strengthen your positive expectations.

Concentrate on a plan you can believe in and focus on and celebrate each one of the small successes – no matter how insignificant they may seem at the time – all along the way. Remember, you can't very well expect others to believe they will succeed if you do not believe it yourself!

Henry Ford said, "If you believe you can or you believe you can't – you're right." Strengthen your belief in the inevitability of your success, expect success and watch out for the powerful leaders you will begin to attract.

In addition to examining your own belief level, look for other qualities that characterize you as a successful leader or an attractive business partner.

Examine the following list to see which of the qualities are ones you now possess. Then, go on to identify those qualities that, if further developed, would enhance your ability to attract others.

A big part of successful prospecting and enrolling is how attractive you are to your prospect as a sponsor and business partner. Phil Knall of Scottsdale, Arizona, is a good example. Confidence, belief in himself and his opportunity, and the ability to transfer that belief to his prospect characterize his conversations. Phil has the gift of listening

50 Qualities of a Successful Leader and Business Partner

Authentic

Disciplined

Charismatic

Focused

Willing to Sacrifice for the Future

Able to Bond with Others

Believable

Visionary

Supportive

Does Not take Rejection

Personally

Inspirational

Confident

Powerful

Enthusiastic

Interested in Personal Growth
    and Development

Vulnerable

Compassionate

Sensitive

Organized

At Peace

Persistent/Consistent

Teachable

Empowers Others

Ambitious

High Level of Physical Energy

Positive, Up-Beat Attitude

Committed

Good Self Image

Positive Expectation

Happy

Works in Partnership

Burning Desire to Succeed

Intuitive

Empathetic

Happy to Serve

Genuinely Humble

Willing to Contribute to Others

Interested in Others

Entrepreneurial

Doesn't Dump Information

Takes Initiative

Good Communication Skills

Has Integrity-can make and
    keep commitments

Is Proactive-takes initiative

Is a Team Player

Follows Up and Follows Through

And, a Good Listener who listens...

    For what's Important ...

    For what's Missing ...

    For what It's Like in the
    Other Person's World ...

    For Contribution ...

    For the Fit ...

    For the Gold ...

to what's important to his prospect or what's missing in their lives while asking questions that create rich possibilities for them. And, he does it with an arrogant charisma that makes people want to join him. Phil enrolled 22 out of the first 25 people he prospected and continues to have the ability to enroll more than 50% of those with whom he speaks.

Assuming that you are prospecting enough people, your tally sheet will reflect positive results if you possess those qualities that are desirable to and valued by others as they consider the viability of the partnership you are offering. Unfortunately, we're usually the last ones to know how we "land" with others – how they perceive us and interpret us and what we say. People tend to be oblivious to facets of themselves that can often be very apparent to everyone else.

For some insight into how we show up for others and how they show up for us, let's examine the art and science of "Listening" in greater detail.

Chapter Five

Listening

I know you understand what you think I said,
But I'm not sure you realize that what you HEARD
is not what I MEANT....

-Michael Smith, from "The Freedom Course"*

Success in network marketing demands the development of your own leadership skills, as well as the ability to develop others as leaders. At the very core of leadership is the ability to master the art of "listening."

Leaders must take responsibility to see to it others really "get" that they have been heard. They must take responsibility for themselves being heard and understood by others, as well.

In any given conversation, it's not the speaking that actually determines the effectiveness of the communication, but the listening.

We must speak in such a way that others can hear what we say, understand it, and be encouraged to action by it AND we can actually listen the very same, creative way.

Effective communications will cause people to shift in their thinking, their actions, from negative to positive and begin to experience the awesome power of their possibilities.

In network marketing, you can take the point of view that what you actually get paid for is having conversations with people. And every conversation is composed of two elements: speaking and listening.

As human beings, we speak as though we are communicating into a void. Obviously, this is not true! The other person hears what we have to say to the extent that she understands, pays attention, agrees with us, etc.

In other words, whether or not what you say has an impact on another person has more to do with them than it does with you! Their listening has been influenced by all of the events, emotions, and biases that have shaped their personality and therefore, their lives.*

As a result of this predisposed listening everyone possesses, you will be effective in your communication only if you can recognize how others are hearing you. When you do that, you can choose to speak in a way which has the most effect on your listener.

We all have our own automatic ways of listening to others. Most of the time, we are not even aware of it. Yet without awareness, you are at the mercy of your listening habits – you "hear" only what fits the patterns and qualities you listen for.

Have you ever spoken with someone who, no matter what you said or even how you said it, made something negative out of what you said? That's their listening.

Your Background Listening
(Automatic & Mechanical)

1. **Looking Good**
   What does he think about me?
   What am I going to say next to impress her?

2. **Taking Things Personally**
   This is about me- not her.
   Is she conning me?
   Is he lying to me?

3. **Validation**
   Does she like or dislike me?
   Does he agree with me?

4. **Being Offended**
   (Has others walking on eggshells)
   To be defensive, you must be listening so as to avoid
   being offended or insulted.

5. **I Already Know That**
   I know what's good for you.
   I know more than you.
   Do it THIS way (my way).

6. **Quick Closure**
   Hurry up.
   Give me the answer NOW.

7. **Resignation**
   I already tried that. It doesn't work.
   It's no use.
   I quit.

8. **Judgment**
   Right/Wrong
   Good/Bad
   Agree/Disagree

9. **Brevity**
   What's your point?
   Where are we going with this?
   When are we going to get there?

Adapted with permission from "The Freedom Foundation" and Mike Smith

To the degree you become aware of how you listen, awesome possibilities begin to appear that didn't show up before. You cannot generate a powerful, positive listening for someone if you don't recognize your own automatic listening.

The previous chart lists nine of the most common automatic listenings in our Western culture. Let's go through each one to see how it might affect your conversations and your productivity in building your networking business. Check to see how many of these "listenings" have your name on them.

Let's explore each of these listenings in more detail.

1. Looking Good
This listening shows up as a preoccupation with what the other person is thinking about you. And it's impossible to hear someone else when your attention is on yourself. People obsessed with looking good are often too busy com-

posing what they will say next to pay attention to someone else's communication. As a result, what is important or necessary to the other person gets overlooked.

This listening can also keep a conversation from being direct and straight-forward by placing "how you appear" ahead of honesty and contribution to the other person. As a leader, the decision is often between looking good or keeping your commitment to serve others.

The "Y" of Leadership

- Looking good
- Being liked
- Taking the easy way out
- Selling them out
- Saying what's convenient

YOU ARE HERE!

- Standing in your commitments
- Risking
- Doing the right thing
- Telling the truth

Which path will you choose?

2. Taking Things Personally

Have you ever thought that it rained, because you just spent two hours washing and waxing your car? That's taking things personally – in the extreme.

In network marketing, this listening might take the form of feeling that you are being rejected, scorned, or otherwise insulted when someone decides not to join your company. It most probably has absolutely nothing to do with you. Perhaps it's just not the right time for that person to get involved. Maybe they're going through a family crisis, a problem with work, or it's a bad time that particular day.

The point is, see if you listen in the way of taking things personally. If you do, are you willing to generate a different interpretation for what you hear? You can do that by realizing that what the other person is saying is about him or her, his opinion, her judgment, his interpretation or unique point of view. It is not about you. Give it a try. Also, learn to recognize the listening habits of those you speak with. If your people tend to take things personally, you might offer alternative interpretations to empower them and teach them to create a new, more positive listening.

3. Validation

Like "Looking Good," listening for validation – or its twin, listening to avoid being invalidated – can severely hamper powerful, straight-forward and empowering communication.

If your listening is "Do they like me?" you'll need to guard against taking the easy way out whenever the prospect of offending someone arises. Those who are overly concerned with validation will make decisions that support being liked over higher, more difficult, choices, such as telling the truth.

Once again, it's the result of having your attention on yourself, not on listening to the other person.

Ask yourself, "Do I want to make a difference, take a stand, contribute – or take the 'easy' way out just to get a little validation?"

4. Being Offended

Do you know anyone who constantly listens for the possibility of being offended? That's a person who, no matter what you say or how you say it, takes offense at something in the conversation.

People with this listening appear to be always "looking for trouble." They're not really happy until they find some slight or insult, something to complain about.

Have you ever talked to someone about joining you in your business and she reacts violently?

Perhaps, she says something like, "What do you mean, establish a second income, there's nothing wrong with my current income! I'm doing great. Don't' tell me I'm working too hard. I like working six days a week. Mind your own business!"

That person expects offensive intentions, no matter what the subject.

If you have this listening, the key to generating a more productive one is to shift your interpretations to ones that empower or support you. Mike Smith teaches us that the easiest way to do this is to distinguish between "what happened" (or what was actually said word-for-word) and what "interpretation" your own mind "made up." People who are easily offended often have these two, very different, realms collapsed into one. They can't tell the difference between the sound of the other person's voice and the noise inside their own mind.

EVENT	vs	STORY
What Happened?		Interpretation

Once you distinguish what actually happened from the interpretation you made up about what happened, you can see clearly which elements are your responsibility, and then generate different, less "negative" and inaccurate interpretations which empower and serve.

So, when a prospect tells you he is not interested in what you have to offer, instead of being insulted by his rejection of you, or his lack of belief in your ability to succeed, shift your interpretation to one that supports you. Maybe he would love to be in business with you, but has no belief in himself. Or perhaps he has some other concern that prevents him from moving forward.

Create an interpretation that moves you forward. Then you can ask questions to see if he is willing to share his reasoning, so that you might support him in his decision.

5. I Already Know

If you're a leader, I'm certain you have this one! It's not that knowing is bad or that being clueless is better. There's value in recognizing that "already knowing the answer" is how you listen, and there's power in remembering to stay open to possibilities.

Without the awareness that you listen as "I already know," you won't recognize value in new and unfamiliar possibilities. You risk writing off good ideas as impossible, simply because they don't conform to your established thinking.

There are three areas of knowledge:

Area 1. What we know.

Area 2. What we don't know.

Area 3. What we don't know that we don't know....

I know how to speak English (Area 1) and I don't know how to speak Greek (Area 2). Very few new possibilities exist for me in either of these two areas. If I apply myself to learn what I don't know, Area 2, it then moves to Area 1, what I do know.

But the greatest potential for growth comes out of Area 3, what I don't know I don't know.

Confusing? Let me explain:

Let's say you don't know how to ride a bicycle.

Now, you have some knowledge about bicycles and riding one from looking at one and watching others ride (Area 1). And you know there's much you don't know; such as the physics and mechanics of the gears and how to use them to climb a hill (Area 2). But "What you don't know you don't know" is balance.

Balance is the key to riding a bike. But until you climb on and successfully ride one, you've got no idea what it's like, no sense of what it's really like to be in or out of balance.

Once you learn, you never forget. But until you got into a position on that bike to explore what you didn't know you didn't know, the discovery of balance was totally outside your realm of reality – almost as if it didn't exist. And for you, it didn't!

That's the awesome power of possibilities in what you don't know you don't know.

When you recognize that you're listening from "I already know," give yourself permission to not know, then listen for new possibilities. Your breakthroughs will come as a result of your willingness to "try on" a new idea or concept, one of which you were not previously aware.

If you are speaking to someone with this listening, you might ask her, "Would you be willing to temporarily put aside any preconceptions you have in order to look objectively and explore any new possibilities that might develop?"

6. Quick Closure

This is a kind of listening that must come up with the answer – fast. A person who listens for quick closure is not willing to make the time to check things out, or explore other angles and possibilities.

The cost of this listening is that much is missed if it is not readily and immediately apparent – and much, if not most, especially when dealing with human beings, is not always clear and concise right away. Quick closure can often lead to imprudent, poor decisions, because they are made in haste.

If you recognize this listening as your own, you would be wise to slow down, manage your need to know the answer right away, and be open to the less visible possibilities.

Someone with this listening may get turned off while you are trying to explain the rules and intricacies of your compensation plan. If she can't get it right away, she's gone.

With such a person you may want to avoid the tedious details of the plan at first, and focus instead on the easier-to-understand concept of how people are paid – just touching on the highlights of the plan, such as achievement levels.

Prospects with this listening will often hang up on you before you've had a chance to explore with them what you have to offer in any detail. Keeping such a prospect engaged in the conversation will require you to create value right up front and right away.

One key here, is to be curious about your prospect. Ask questions that reveal your interest in her, and constantly ask her to "Tell me more about that." And lead with the benefits. That will keep up your prospect's self-interest.

7. Resignation

Listening with resignation shuts down all those new ideas which can be linked in any way to one or more past failures.

A good example of listening with resignation is the prospect who tried MLM 15 years ago without success and is now resigned to the "fact" that "these things don't work." For that person, network marketing is not a possibility. MLM equals failure, and he is resigned to that "truth." Resignation kills the life force of enthusiasm in people.

Young children are generally open to all new challenges and possibilities. As years pass, the sea of resignation rises to drown them in negative possibilities. Those who listen with resignation are comfortable with the reasons things can't be done and shouldn't even be attempted.

The most effective antidote for resignation is training yourself to generate conversations for possibilities: i.e., conversations about your dreams, inspirations, desires, goals and aspirations.

Like any weak muscle, such conversations will probably seem awkward and strained at first, but it's quite conceivable to train yourself to create possibilities as a matter of habit. It is this ability to ALWAYS look for possibilities in

EVERY situation that will generate the vitality and energy that will surely result in your successful action.

As you're prospecting, you may often encounter resignation such as, "I'm too busy to learn something new.... I'm too old to start over.... Only other people could succeed at that."

Pick an excuse, any excuse. They're all variations on hopelessness. As a networker, it is your happy obligation to inspire hope in other people, and the attitude that anything is possible with partnership, determination and the willingness to succeed.

8. Judging

This listening is, sadly, an inbred part of our society and culture. We judge everything as better or worse, right or wrong, good or bad. And we either agree or disagree with it!

The problem with this is that if you agree with something, you must already know it and have used it to get where you are now. There's nothing new, nothing to be learned, nothing there to take you to the next higher level. In short, no progress.

If you disagree, you rule it out as having any value without giving it another thought. As a result, this listening, too, tends to stifle any new possibilities for you.

With the listening of "Judgment," and other automatic listenings, recognize when you are listening in a way which inhibits you. Choose whether or not that is what you really want. And if not, then generate a more powerful listening to better support your efforts.

The challenge when you encounter a prospect who listens in this way is to create the opening of trying on something new, exploring it as if he's learning it for the very first time.

You might ask, "Would you be willing to put aside everything you think you already know about what I'm going to say, and evaluate it with a fresh, open mind? I'm convinced you'll find this (exciting, interesting, valuable, etc.) And if it doesn't work for you, you can always continue to think the way you did before. Is that fair enough?"

9. Brevity

Any of you that couldn't wait until I finished with this list have this listening. "Hurry up. Get to the point. Where are you going with all this?"

Type A personalities – especially from the Northeast (I say from personal experience) – have this listening for brevity. The problem comes when speaking with someone who speaks slowly and deliberately (maybe a Southern Type B). Before the Southern B can get to the valuable point, Northern A is off somewhere else, having dismissed the conversation as worthless due to its slow pace.

If you find yourself listening impatiently for the bottom line, manage your concentration to stay present and engaged, looking for value – value which will likely come as a direct result of your patience.

In addition to these nine automatic types, you will surely discover variations and combinations that describe your own particular listening. To the extent that you can clearly identify how you listen, you will be able to change when you choose. You will be able to generate, when needed, a more powerful listening to better support your relationships and goals.

Your automatic listening is the filter through which you see the world. If you alter this filter by shifting how you interpret things, you will change the actions that result. And by altering your actions in this way, you'll affect your productivity dramatically.

Your success in networking can take place only when people are open to listening to what you have to say, once you've established a connection or bond with them. You can further enhance this bond by generating more powerful conversations based upon listening in ways which honor and empower other people.

Generating a Powerful Listening

Now that you have an idea of how you automatically listen to others, let's see how you can develop a more effective, creative listening to support your networking relationships.

The following are listenings you can create in the moment, which will empower you and your prospects.

1. Listening to appreciate what it is like in the other person's world.

If everyone had the same background, interests, income, and beliefs, our government and economy would be simple. And, we would all work for one huge MLM company.

Life would also be terminally boring.

Every prospect is unique. That is what makes them challenging, valuable, and full of possibility. Pay attention to the differences as well as the common ground, and respect the other person's perspective. Not only will you hear new ways you can contribute to your prospect's life, you will learn the special strengths your prospect has to offer.

2. **Listening for concerns, commitments, and values.**

This will provide you with direct access to ways your company can enhance the lives of your prospects.
Listen first, then offer your company's possibilities.

Does your prospect prize family time above everything else?

Is your prospect worried about environmental, social, or political issues?

These are examples of core issues, which also relate to time and money.

Does your business promote working from home (no polluting commute) with flexible time for family events? If there was enough time and money in the opportunity, would it allow your prospect to volunteer for a favorite charity?

3. **Listening for the gold.**

Sadly, most people usually listen for the dirt. But what if you approached every conversation believing "everyone has something to contribute to me – a different style or viewpoint to expand my mind and experience." How would your conversation be enhanced by your certainty, going in, that gold nuggets were just waiting there for you to find them?

Generate this kind of listening (even with people you

don't really consider to be particularly powerful or insightful) and I guarantee you will never be disappointed with what you gain from the conversation. Take the attitude that every conversation you have is meant to contribute at least one insight. With this expectation, your listening will be tuned in for, and inevitably begin to attract, something of value every time.

4. Listening for what's at stake (for yourself and for others).

This is a particularly powerful and productive listening. If you have something "at stake" in each conversation, you are sure to come away with much, much more than if you go into the dialogue as a disinterested observer. Think about how you listen to the typical preflight safety instructions routinely given on an airplane before take-off. Would you be more attentive if you were told, mid-flight, that the engines had failed and the plane was going down? Listening with something at stake will get you infinitely more from your conversations.

Likewise, if you listen for what is at stake for others, you will readily know where to direct your conversation to explore how you might contribute to their lives.

As you prospect, listen to what's at stake for the other person: is it their family's survival, the satisfaction they long for in their job, their happiness, or maybe simply the "possibility" of a lifestyle with more time or money?

5. Listening for Possibility

This is perhaps the richest listening of all.

Most people tend to quickly rule out possibilities (probably because of listening with resignation). In network marketing, people usually say "No" either from a fear of commitment, or because the possibilities are simply not rich and rewarding enough.

If every prospect knew what you know about your opportunity, would they get in and join you?

Of course they would. If that's true, then your job is simply to help prospects explore their possibilities fully, so they can make an informed decision – right? And that gives a whole new possibility to the prospecting conversation.

Most people hesitate to look for possibilities, because they fear being obligated to take on more responsibility. First create and then communicate the opportunity for them to look into the possibilities without having to make a commitment to anything other than making an exploration.

When you generate a listening for possibilities, new options open up which naturally help people get past their fears, stops and breakdowns. Often, from a completely unrelated, even "bizarre" idea, a new and exciting possibility appears. The more freedom people experience to explore possibilities, the more opportunities will show up for them in the process.

Here's the key:

Whatever you listen for shapes your reality.

By having the courage to listen proactively and with the expectation of positive results, you will have miracles show up all around you. Nothing – positive or negative – can show up unless you create the listening for it. And it's a scientific fact, people respond to whatever listening we provide for them.

Recent studies actually show a link between physical health and being listened to. When a person feels listened to, the cilia – the microscopic hairlike process – that line the inner ear are stimulated. They trigger the brain to release endorphins, which exert a beneficial physiological effect.

When we generate an expanded, positive listening for others, we literally create a world of new possibilities for them. To generate such a powerful listening only takes your intention to do so, AND recognizing when you are not acting on that intention.

The key to successfully building a large network marketing organization is in your listening. Success begins in the listening you provide for your prospects and the listening you provide for the men and women in your organization. True partnership finds its source in the generation of a powerful listening. This listening is also the basis for the shift in the way networking is and will be conducted in the new millennium.

It no longer works to simply share information. Relationships are now the key. Create a true bond with people. Listen to their concerns and to what's most important in their lives. Contribute. Explore their possibilities. This is what the shift is about.

---

*This chapter on "Listening" is dedicated to my two coaches and mentors, Carol McCall and Mike Smith. Both are experts on "Listening" and much of the information presented here is sourced in their work. For more on the topic, please see my books, *The Power to Succeed: 30 Principles for Maximizing Your Personal Effectiveness* and *The Power to Succeed: More Principles for Powerful Living, Book II.*

Chapter Six

Creating a Structure for Personal Development

Once you have identified those qualities and areas of listening to develop for yourself, you'll need to create a structure for that process. Without a system to continually work on yourself, it's all too easy to slip back into those old, comfortable habits you wanted to change.

One of your goals here must be to design a structure that will promote and support feedback in the critical area of your on-going personal evaluation.

There are countless ways for you to get feedback to develop your enrolling and sponsoring skills. Recording your phone conversations and having them critiqued by a mentor, asking your prospects for feedback after a conversation, keeping a contact log to gauge your progress where you rate your developing skills and look for what's missing.... Every one of these options provides valuable information on how others experience you.

Choose a Mentor or Coach

When Olympic athletes put themselves in training to develop their skills and improve their performance, the first thing they do is hire a coach. Likewise, as you develop yourself in any of the areas that will contribute to your business-building success, it is imperative that you select one or more people who will champion your efforts, provide you with valuable feedback, and serve as additional resources for increasing your business success and personal growth. These people are your coaches and mentors.

How many coaches and mentors should you have?

As many as possible. The only limit is the time you make to be in contact with them.

As you select your mentors, or your "hot team" of coaches, select those people who you perceive possess the qualities you wish to develop and strengthen. Be very specific in requesting how they can support you: by listening, giving feedback, instruction, etc. Enroll your coaching team into your vision and share with them those areas of self-development you've chosen to focus on.

Setting Up the Game

Commit to a certain number of quality prospecting conversations (by phone or in person) over the course of the next 60 days. Make your goal here a stretch. You need to have enough conversations to gain the optimum benefit in the shortest possible time. As an example, commit to, say, 100 contacts over this two-month period.

Make a List and Work On It Daily

To begin, select one to five qualities which you will

develop. List those qualities in as much detail as possible on a 3x5 index card. Carry this card with you everywhere, reviewing it regularly and reading it before you engage in each conversation with others.

After each conversation, and at the end of each day, rate yourself on a scale from one to ten as to how you did with regard to the quality you are developing. Use a benchmark by selecting something you said or did that was a "10," and then rate your performance in that one area against that standard. If you don't have a "perfect 10" to relate to, make up an example of you being excellent in one area and use that for comparison.

Always ask yourself: What worked? What was missing? What could be improved upon in your next conversation? Here's an example of what I mean:

If the quality you are working on is showing enthusiasm to others, rate yourself on the degree of enthusiasm you conveyed to your prospect.

- Did she understand that you love what you do?
- Was it clear to him that you're succeeding, and can transfer that success to him when he joins you?
- What worked about your energy?
- Was anything lacking with respect to enthusiastically conveying the benefits you had to offer her?

Go through a similar self-examination with each of the other qualities you are working to develop and strengthen. Remember, there are no weaknesses. Only strengths you have yet to develop. That's just one more example of the

Awesome Power of Possibilities you always have – to constantly improve yourself in some way each and every day!

Keep a Journal

Purchase a bound notebook like the sketch books artists use. Make it attractive so you're pleased and proud to carry it with you. Write in it all the areas you plan to develop to make you a more powerful communicator, sponsor, enroller and so on. Have that list in the very front of your journal. Leave about twenty pages blank to have room for future areas of development. Start today and record all of your conversations on a daily basis.

Record the highlights of your conversations. Number each one. Include the date. Indicate the person's name, occupation, and how you came to speak with him or her (referral, ad lead, friend, etc.). Keep notes on all the unique and unusual elements of your conversation.

Record what's important or missing in your prospect's life. If they are stressed out at work, make a note of it. Not enough money to put the kids through college; they hate their job; no free time. Write it all down.

What were their objections?

How did the conversation end?

What's the next action for you?

What's the next action for them?

What worked about each conversation?

What was missing that, if put into place, would make you more effective in the future?

Some examples of what could be missing follow:

- Listening ...
- Being Focused ...
- Being Organized ...
- Being Powerful ...
- Having Courage ...
- Being Persistent ...
- Being Confident ...
- Handling Objections ...
- Your Belief Level ...
- Being Enthusiastic ...
- Conveying Positive Energy ...
- Not Arguing ...
- Not Interrupting ...
- Creating the Space for Your Prospect to Make a Choice ...

The level of your development and the speed at which you grow will often be directly related to the quality of the questions you ask yourself. Here are some examples:

Did I establish sufficient rapport?

Did I speak more than I listened?

Did I find out what was important to my prospect?

Did I find out what was missing in my prospect's life?

Did I uncover their "seeds of discontent?"

Did I dump information?

Did I pressure my prospect?

Did I guide the conversation and move it forward?

Was I discerning and decisive?

Would I find myself attractive as a sponsor, a business partner?

Did I generate an empowering listening for my prospect?

Did I make my prospect wrong?

Did I honor my prospect's values?

Did I connect my prospect's passions with the opportunity?

Did I see how I could contribute to my prospect's life?

You will need to design debriefing questions like the ones above which address those areas that can create the most leverage for your success. As your conversations progress, new questions will emerge and previously hidden areas of development will be added to your list.

Track your progress and notice how, as you develop certain traits, others begin to show up as possible future areas of development. Have and track 100 different conversations as you critique yourself in each area.

You will notice (as will others) a continued and marked improvement as you exercise these new muscles. Just like working out in the gym, you may feel sore at first. For many of you, this will be a brand new process. Yes, it is hard work, I know. But you WILL see results, and you WILL see them more quickly than you can imagine. It is simply impossible to engage in this process and not develop and grow tremendously, and fast, too.

I have never met one person who has taken on this process who has not gotten stunning results almost immediately – not one!

Remember, personal growth and development is never "handled." It's all too easy to revert to old habits if you stop developing and maintaining new and better ones. Remind yourself constantly to keep on your course of constant and never-ending improvement.

Three-Way Calls With Your Coaches

An excellent way to get feedback on how others are perceiving you, is to have a third party listen to your conversations with the intent of giving you constructive criticism.

Have your coaches tell you what worked, what was missing, and how you could be more effective in your communication. Get input on how successfully you communicated the traits you're working to strengthen.

Audio Tape feedback

Purchase an inexpensive cassette recorder and a telephone line recording device from your local electronics store. Record your conversations with the intent of getting specific feedback from your coaches.

With audio tapes, your coaches can critique your calls at their convenience. You also can review them, too, and see how you sounded to your prospects and discover how you could improve your communication in the future.

Get Your Prospect's Feedback

At times, it may be appropriate to get direct input from your prospects on what it is like for them to interact with you. This feedback is particularly appropriate from people with whom you have developed rapport – those who know you and those who are willing to contribute to your development process.

Just be direct and ask.

One of my favorite questions to start with is, "What did you like best about the conversation?" That way, you start off with a positive.

A great next question is, "What was missing from the conversation which would have made it better (more clear, more powerful, more interesting, etc.) for you?"

Put Yourself Into a Personal Development Program

Stepping into the leadership of a rapidly growing networking organization demands that you increase your effectiveness with people. What's more, your organization will likely only grow as fast as you do in your personal development.

Reading books on how to improve your communication and people skills, listening to audio tapes and attending courses to expand who you are are all critical.

Two programs I wholeheartedly endorse are Mike Smith's "Freedom Course" and Carol McCall's "Listening Course." Both programs serve as a solid foundation to begin to examine how you see the world and others and equally importantly how they see you. As we begin to identify areas in which we are limited in terms of our effectiveness with others, new opportunities for breakthroughs begin to open up for us. And our personal growth can only contribute to an increase in productivity in our business and main relationships.

How to Develop Yourself Powerfully
Here's the key question: Are you an attractive business partner and sponsor?

- Identify qualities of a successful leader/business partner
- List five qualities you will need to develop to be the best you can be
- Create a structure for developing yourself
    1) Work on your list daily
    2) Keep a journal
    3) Make three-way calls with your sponsor
    4) Listen to audio tape of your conversations
    5) Listen to prospect feedback on your presentations
    6) Rate yourself after every conversation

Let's look at some other ways to enhance your prospecting effectiveness.

Chapter Seven

The Zen of Prospecting

There are two Zen rules I suggest you must always keep in front of yourself. In fact, these rules are outlined on a sign I keep right by my phone for every prospecting call. For me, they sum up successful prospecting perfectly.

Rule #1: Give up the right to make
anyone do anything.

Rule #2: Look for a way to contribute to
your prospect's life.

Simply following these two simple rules takes away any inclination to exert pressure on your prospect. In network marketing, pressure and intimidation do not work!

A prospect who unwillingly signs up as a distributor – under pressure, or anything other than making an informed choice – will never be motivated to do what it takes to succeed. What may look like a victory in the short term will turn out to be a waste of time and energy if your reluctant prospect needs you to constantly push and pull them into action.

By giving up the right to make anyone do what you want them to do, you create the space for them to step forward powerfully and freely choosing their actions to succeed.

And that's where Rule #2 comes into play.

The real power of network marketing lies in its positive impact on peoples' lives.

Network marketing is about contribution.

Everyone has some aspect of their life where your opportunity can contribute something of value. For many, it may be a supplemental monthly paycheck. For others, it may be complete financial and time freedom, or the opportunity to contribute to the lives of others. If you look hard enough and ask the right questions, you'll usually discover just where your contribution fits.

As for those who see absolutely nothing of value in what you could contribute to their lives – the opportunity is simply not right for them at this time. Let it be. It's not up to you to force a fit.

Finding Out Who Your Prospect Is

The key to any successful relationship, is developing a bond with the other person, establishing a common ground, the mutuality that will allow the two of you to communicate and function as partners. This bond includes permission to explore the possibilities of involvement in that partnership.

All too often, the first prospecting instinct is to dump information. Distributors often feel, "Just one more fact or tidbit about my company, my products, or my opportunity will be the one thing that makes the difference – the thing that gets them in!" So, they tell the prospect everything they know, hoping to persuade her to see the same value that attracted them.

This is a very blind approach. You have no clue what would interest another person – unless you ask. So instead, we rely on dumping information on deaf ears.

Stephen Covey advises in his book, *The Seven Habits of Highly Effective People*, "Seek first to understand, then to be understood."

You can't possibly be effective in meeting the needs and wants of others if you don't know what they are! Get to know your prospects first. Step into their shoes. Walk a mile or two. Find out what it's like to live and work in their world.

Once you've listened "to understand" who they are, you will have created the space for them to listen to your presentation and for you "to be understood."

Have you heard the cliché, "People don't' care how much you know until they know how much you care?" Listen to people and you will create the opening for them to listen to you. Human beings nearly always honor the Golden Rule: They will do unto you as you do unto them.

Building Rapport

Bill DiPietro is a mild mannered, unassuming, even shy

kind of a guy. He's also built a huge networking organization with more than a dozen strong leader legs. And he's done it by building rapport. In fact, he's a master at building rapport. Bill will tell you that his success is a direct result of getting to know his prospects, speaking to them heart to heart and after he has created a connection (then and only then) share something about his company, products and opportunity. Bill becomes a friend first – then a possible business partner with something of value to contribute based upon his rapport-building conversation.

If you remember only one thing about successful prospecting-this is it: Rapport must precede the exchange of information.

A casual conversation is the best way to build this rapport. In other words, find out what you can about people before you share your opportunity.

Here's how to prevent your prospecting conversations from ever being a FLOP.

Simply remember to ask about the following:

> F- Family
> L- Live
> O- Occupation
> P- Passions

F- Family

This is one thing most people are willing to talk about – especially their kids. Make the opportunity to ask about their family. Show curiosity and a sincere interest in what is most important to them. This is particularly a good starting point to reestablish rapport with people you already know, but have been out of touch with for a while. Asking "How's your family?" is the best way to build an instant bond.

L- Live

With strangers, this is the best place to start. Everyone has to live somewhere. Look for points of interest regarding a favorite region, hometown, or current residence. Even people who come from a not-so-great place can be proud of their roots.

A great ice breaker on an airplane is, "Are you leaving home or going home today?" It's easy from there. After all, we all live on the same common ground.

O- Occupation

Most people spend many hours and a great deal of energy on their work – whether they like it or not! This is one of the easiest places to explore when speaking to a stranger or deepening an acquaintance, after you've opened up where they are form or currently live. For example: "Where are you from?" "Dallas." "Oh, what do you do there?" And so on.

Questions such as, "How long have you been doing that?" or responses like, "Really, tell me more about that...," give the person an opportunity to speak about themselves – which is usually their favorite subject!

This line of questioning also allows you to explore their level of satisfaction with their work.

I'll often ask people, "What do you like best about your work?" And then, "What do you enjoy the least?" I've learned over the years to start off on the positive. If there are negatives, they'll come out sooner or later.

Other conversation options might be, "How many days a week do you work?" "Do you do much traveling?" One of my favorites is, "Let's say that money is no object, all your bills are paid, your kids' tuition's handled, etc. Would you still do what you're doing for a living now? Would you work less or not at all?" "What would you do in your spare time?"

P - Passions (as reflected in hobbies, recreation and special interests)

This is where you look for the gold. These are the things that people get excited about telling you.

Do they love to travel? If so, where would they go? With whom? Golf? How often would they play? Maybe they like to paint or fish or bird watch. It doesn't matter what it is they love to do. What matters is that through a conversation with you they begin to dream.

As they share their dreams, they realize that they just don't have the time or the money to do what they'd like. That's where you and your opportunity come in with the awesome power of possibilities.

Don't rush at this point. Let them get it all out. Encourage them: "Tell me more about that... What's that like for you... How do you feel when you're ...?

Being a contribution requires two things: Knowing what you're contributing – and patience. (Remember Zen Rule #2)

To summarize, find out who your prospects are. Each person has unique reasons for being attracted to your opportunity. It's much more effective to find out their reasons for doing your opportunity, rather than you giving them yours.

Look for what they value most. What's important to them and what's missing in their lives and work?
Talk in terms of possibilities. Explore their dreams, wants, and aspirations.

Guide the conversation with questions designed to have them speak about themselves.

Explore the "seeds of discontent" in their lives. Is it money they lack, or time to spend with family and friends? Is it their job that they hate, or the lack of substantial savings for retirement? Maybe there isn't a lot of fun in their daily routine. Is their stress level so high that their health and happiness are likely to suffer?

Whatever it is, you won't discover it by doing all the talking. Ask a question – then shut up and listen. Listen without judgment. Listen wide open. Your one and only job is to hear what they say.

98 out of 100 people haven't been listened to and truly heard in years! What do you suppose they will think and feel about you if you're the one person who actually listens to them...?

If you find yourself speaking more than listening, reevaluate your approach.

What are you listening for?

Most importantly, how and where can you be a contribution to their lives...?

What Do You Say?

The particular approach to prospecting you use will depend upon the person you're speaking with, how you know them, and what you think and feel would be appropriate to say to fit their interests. Some examples of approaches worth considering follow:

A. "I'm involved in a new, exciting enterprise and I'm interviewing for business partners. I was wondering if you'd be willing to take a look at the possibilities with me and see if there might be something here for you?

B. "I want to run something by you and get your feedback. I'm working with some very successful business people to expand our company in this region. I'm helping them to set up interviews this week in their search for local partners. Would you be willing to take a look at what we've got?"

C. "I've begun a home-based business with the help of some very successful entrepreneurs. Do you know anyone who might be interested in making an extra $2,000 to $5,000 per month working with me as a business partner?"

D. "Do you know any (insert the specific occupation, such as doctor, lawyer, Indian chief...)? I'm in partnership with a group of (occupation again), and we're working on expanding locally (or nationally)."

E. "(Name),I want to run something by you. I respect your opinion and would like to get some feedback."

F. "You mentioned (area of career concern or discontent). If I could show you a way to double your present income, yet still have more free time over the next two to four years, would you be interested in taking a look at it with me?"

G. "Would an extra $___ per month be of interest to you?" (Estimate their current income and divide by two.)

H. (As a product approach.) "You mentioned a problem with _____. I have a product that might help."

You can see that there are almost an infinite number of ways to begin a prospecting conversation. The previous examples were not for prospects responding to an ad. Advertising respondents require a somewhat different approach.

One way to approach an ad lead would be: introduce yourself briefly and determine if this is a good time for your prospect to talk. If it is, say something like, "I would be happy to tell you a little bit about our company, opportunity, and product line. Would it be OK if I asked you a few questions first to see where your interest lies?" Ask a few questions about what they do, why they responded to your ad, where their interest lies, etc., all the while building rapport and friendship.

At this point, you can briefly explain about your opportunity or products. Speak in terms of what makes your company unique and special. You might then ask if they would be interested in reading some literature, watching a video, or listening to an audio tape, depending on what your company is using successfully?

Your Networking Sequence

Step 1
1. Make acquaintances, break the ice, start a friendship.
2. Build rapport- (Remember FLOP).
3. Listen for what's important and what's missing.
4. Ask the qualifying question:
   "Would you be interested if I could show you a way to
   _____ (and fill in the blank with their 'Why')?"

Interested?

If "Yes" Step 2	or	If "No" Step 2
Send/Give a Prospecting Pack		1. Suggest being a retail customer.
		2. Ask for referrals.
		3. Go on to the next prospect.

Still Interested?

If "Yes"	If "Maybe"	If "No"
(go below)	Follow Up	(go above to Step 2)
	(send additional material pertinent	
	to the prospect, for example, an	
	audio tape, product brochure,	
	compensation plan, etc.)	
	Additional Follow-up until you get a	

"Yes"	"Maybe"	"No"
Go to Step 4	Additional Follow-up	(go above to Step 2)

Step 3-If the answer is "Yes"
Do a 3-way presentation with upline

Still interested?

Step 4- If the answer is "Yes"- Enrollment
1. Fill out Paperwork
2. Introduce to all Products
3. Introduce New Person to upline

Step 5- Get Started Training
1. Work in partnership to develop a vision
2. Develop a Game Plan
3. Follow your Company's System

Ask direct questions that forward the action of the conversation to its next step – like setting up a follow up appointment or a three-way call.

Having covered these preliminary areas in the prospecting process, you have now determined whether your prospect has an interest in exploring what you have to offer, or not. If they're interested, let's proceed to your next step....

What information do you send your prospect?

Sorting Packages

Your prospect is interested. He's willing to evaluate some information on what you're offering. So, what do you send him?

Avoid the temptation to make a rookie distributor mistake by sending your prospect everything you can get your hands on! The tendency is to think that one more piece of literature, or reprint, or article, or booklet, or audio, or video will surely make the difference that brings them into the business.

It never does!

Keep Your Sorting Package Simple!

Whenever possible, stick to professionally-produced materials put out by your company expressly for this purpose. Avoid sending a barrage of quickly-made photocopies that make a negative statement about you or your company's image of quality.

A typical sorting package might include:

1. A personalized (one page) cover letter from you.

2. An Enrollment brochure or brochure on your product line.

3. Company-produced literature pertinent to your prospect's interests.

4. An audio or video tape – if available and appropriate to your prospect.

(If your company has several product lines targeting several different groups, select the line most likely to be of interest to your prospect.)

5. A product sample – again, if appropriate.

(This is optional. I often suggest omitting the product sample, as I don't want to make my products the issue. Remember, your main product is your business opportunity.)

The completeness and extent of your package will likely depend upon your prospects' perceived level of interest. When in doubt, send just enough to arouse curiosity and stimulate interest in his learning more. Of course, it is often advisable to start out by suggesting that your prospect visit your website as a first step to determine their level of interest.

The Sorting Conversation

Your prospects have received your company's package and are interested in exploring more. They are now ready for the "sorting conversation."

Sorting is the process of determining if a prospect is interested in becoming a retail customer, a wholesale customer, and/or a distributor. It is a quality conversation during which your prospect gets to explore the details and benefits of the different things you have to offer.

A sorting conversation can be directed toward product, or opportunity, or both. I like to stress the benefits of the business opportunity, but your prospect must understand that your opportunity is founded on an outstanding product line. Just don't forget that your opportunity is in fact your most exciting product of all!

For some people, it may be easier to focus on product first. Often, excitement over the results your prospect gets from using your product may encourage them to explore the opportunity with you.

If you've already discovered a strong interest in the concept of building a business, you will want to focus there first. If you're unsure of their interest, stress the product benefits first to build credibility for your opportunity presentation.

Remember ...
When you STRESS PRODUCTS you'll attract CUSTOMERS.
When you STRESS OPPORTUNITY you attract
    ENTREPRENEURS.
When you STRESS VISION you attract LEADERS....

Start product conversations by firmly establishing the benefits of their use. Look to direct the focus of the conversation toward the opportunity that the products make possible. And taking this one step further, support your prospect in exploring a vision of what the opportunity – fueled by the products – might look like for them.

Ask specific questions that get them to dream.

"What if...?" is a great way to get your prospect to explore the awesome power of possibilities available through your particular networking opportunity.

Share BENEFITS first and then support them with features.

Stress the unique appeal of your products based on the results they can achieve for the prospect. What distinguishes your products from all the others on the market? Tell personal stories that illustrate and support your claims. Remember – facts tell, but stories sell!

Get to know and be able to share how other people have been positively affected by your products and the opportunity they provide. Explain what sets your company apart from all the rest. Why are you so proud to be associated with them? Emphasize awards, accolades, positive press coverage and the honors and recognition your company has received. Accumulate and share powerful press releases, articles and stories about your company and its people. And always, invite your prospect to dream of what might be possible if ....

Present a Plan For Your Prospect's Success

This step is crucial!

Without easily understanding just how they will be able to make the opportunity work for them, your prospects will have real reservations about getting involved. It is your job to help them practically envision their success.

The easiest way to communicate this vision is with a proven plan that outlines the concept of geometric progression. It doesn't really matter what the plan is – it only matters that ...

1. **It's easy to understand.**
2. **It's easy to teach to others.**
3. **It's believable.**

A plan is only a tool to guide your distributor into action. No one's organization will end up resembling the geometric progressions of a specific plan or model. And it doesn't matter, as long as the plan stimulates the level of belief needed to fuel your distributor's action.

Any plan must first take into consideration the compensation structure of the company, and then answer the following questions:

1. How many people will I need to prospect and over what time period?
2. Where will I get their names? (warm market lists, advertisements, cold calls, etc.)
3. How many first, second, and third line/level leaders will I need to develop to earn the income I desire?
4. How much volume will my organization need to generate to yield this income level?

To illustrate, let's look at a plan to earn $15,000 per month. Sketched out by generations, it might look like:

YOU

1. Sponsor six people that
   - Use the products
   - Recommend them

- Sponsor others

2. Help them each sponsor six that
   - Use the products
   - Recommend them
   - Sponsor others

3. Help your six help their six to do the same.

	Network Total
You sponsor six	6
Who sponsor six	36
Who sponsor six	216
Who sponsor six	1296

Resulting in 1554 people in your network.

IF-

1. They each average $100 per month in product volume

2. You earn an average of 10 percent commission on all sales

3. You would earn ...

**1554 People x $100 Monthly Volume x 10%
Average Commission = $15,540 per month**

This plan shows a new distributor (or prospect) that they would need to find only six front line leaders, each willing to find six more leaders, and so forth for four generations in all.

The next place to look is, "How many people would you need to prospect to come up with these six?" If you estimate that you may need to speak with 100 people before you find one leader, you would then need to speak with 600 prospects to get those six leaders.

If you want to have your six first generation leaders in place within six months, you will need on average to speak with 100 prospects each month for that time. If you prospect 20 days per month, you would then need to speak with five people each day to be on track.

So, where will you get you five people each day – ads, acquaintances, associates, cold calling?

As you can see, this illustration gives your new distributor a starting point for action. He must understand that he will continually need to analyze these ratios and adjust them to the actual success rates he is experiencing.

Creare a Recruiting Explosion with the SWAT Team Approach

In building a successful network marketing business, massive action generates massive results. And there is no better time to get your new distributors off to a good start in developing habits that will support their success than their first 30 days in the business. Try this swat team approach with your next enthusiastic new distributor and watch her business (and yours) take off like a rocket as a result.

The concept is a simple one. You offer to partner with your new distributor to create in partnership with them an organization of a solid leg containing 10 distributors in their first 30 days in the business. You then duplicate this plan to produce 4 solid legs with each leg having at least 10 distributors in each one – over the next 4 months. With such a solid base to begin your new front line partner's MLM career, you will have created a positive expectation for future success while establishing a winning work ethic. Secrets to the plan's success include:

1. Everyone enrolls as an independent distributor and commits to a monthly automatic order (usually about $100) for a minimum of 4 months to give the program enough time to work.

2. You, as the new person's sponsor commit to doing their first ten presentations with them over the next 7 days or less. They agree NOT to do these presentations alone until they have done their first 10 with you.

3. They agree to put you in front of ten people (in person preferably or by telephone) with whom they have credibility and to whom they wish to contribute the gift of success.

4. You do a 3-way presentation for their first prospect. You explain that you have committed to supporting your business partner to succeed very rapidly in building a successful networking business. Briefly cover what network marketing is – if they are not familiar with the concept. Explain the concept of geometric progression as the doubling effect (take a penny on day 1 and double it every day for 30 days and you'll end up with a sum in the millions). Explain a little about your company and it's product lines. Explain that

your commitment is to have 10 people enrolled within your partner's organization within the next 30 days. You are now both offering to support the prospect in being at the top of an organization of 10 people in thirty days and continuing onward thereafter.

5. You continue to drive the leg deep by working the names list of the newest person that enrolls. So, if you and your front line distributor (A) enroll person (B), you all then devote your energies to supporting person (B) to have 10 new distributors in their first 30 days. As you enroll distributor (C) under (B), you now turn to working with (C)'s names list...and so forth.

6. After you have done 10 3-way presentations, it's time for distributor (A) to start doing 3-ways with their new people.

7. This training duplicates downline, creating an ever expanding group of distributors that become leaders of their own organization, empowering others to develop leaders as well.

8. Before you enroll a 2nd front line distributor to you, you work with your first front line distributor to have at least a downline of 10 people. Each new emerging leader does the same with their group.

9. As long as you are put in front of new people by your downline person, you work their names list with them in partnership. If you have additional time to work your business beyond doing 3 ways with your new distributors, then you work your own names list in order to build a 2nd, then a 3rd leg for yourself - and so forth. Everyone commits to this same condition.

10. Your goal is to have at least 10 new distributors in one leg within 30 days, all of which are on automatic order.

11. In month #2 and in subsequent months, you start the process over again, ideally creating 6 legs in 6 months with each leg containing at least 10 distributors on automatic order.

Keys to the Plan's Success

1. Work with people who trust you. People you have credibility with. Do not rule out or prejudge anyone.

2. Set up your first 10 appointments as soon as possible to create all-important momentum. Aim for 10 appointments in 2 to 7 days.

3. Sign them up (and their prospects) on the spot if possible with a 3-way call to your company or by faxing in their paperwork. Provide your new partners with the necessary support materials until their own come in.

4. Work with your new people by scheduling a weekly bridge teleconference call.

By creating massive action, momentum and enthusiasm will result in a rapidly growing organization that others will want to be a part of. Like any plan, your actual organization will not exactly resemble the plan. However, the enthusiasm and momentum that will be generated will cause a number of on-fire leaders to step forward and launch your organization toward success.

The "Visionary Plan"

We developed this plan for our organization to support our distributors in having a simple, duplicable turnkey system to promote. It's a business plan to earn at least $10,000 per month after 12 months by following the guidelines based on the following two principles:

1. Distributors will succeed only when they prospect a sufficient number of people.

2. Prospects will be attracted only when they have easy access to developing a substantial names list and a sample plan to follow.

The Plan

1. Enroll as a distributor: Sign up for a $100 per month automatic product order from "the company" and a $200 per month ad campaign slot (provided and coordinated by your upline).

2. Call each ad lead/prospect to begin the rapport process. Send a "company approved" sorting packet to the serious leads generated from the ad campaign. This provides your prospect with all the information she needs to evaluate the opportunity as attractive.

3. Prospect at least 100 new people each month, supplementing your ad campaign leads with prospects from other sources.

4. Enroll one new distributor – on a $100 product auto order plus $200 ad campaign slot each month – who commits to following the same plan: i.e., to enroll one new distributor each month, who commits to do the same.

This plan is designed for everyone to succeed. Everyone can substitute $100 worth of consumable products they would ordinarily buy from the store each month with their company's products. The $200 ad campaign ensures a steady flow of new, interested prospects. A commitment to prospect at least 100 new people each month further ensures that enough conversations take place to bring in at least one new business-builder per month.

The force of geometric progression ensures a substantial organization over the next 12 months, providing an income of more than $10,000 per month in one year's time.

The success of the plan is due to its simplicity. No one gets front-loaded with an excessive inventory of product. Anyone can enroll at least one person per month when in such a high level of activity. And the plan is conservative, since it doesn't even consider those distributors who order more than $100 of product monthly, or those who enroll more than one new person to follow the plan each month.

Again, it doesn't matter what the plan is as long as it provides distributors with a way to get into action and the belief that they will succeed as long as they follow the plan.

Follow-Up, Follow-Up, Follow-Up!

You've prospected, sorted, sent information. Now, don't let it all be for naught by not following up! This is where the mountain of gold lies.

Whenever possible, set your follow-up appointment with your prospect before you even mail any materials! Allow two to seven days, depending upon your prospect's specific time commitment to review your materials. Always let your prospect know what the next step is and set it up in advance with their agreement.

Never assume that your prospect is not interested simply because you are unable to reach her for follow-up. What you may interpret as no interest may simply be the challenges of daily life interfering with your prospect's schedule. I can remember countless times when it took six or more attempts to connect with a prospect who was interested, but got distracted somewhere along the way.

Follow up until you get a "Yes," a "No," or a "Try me at a later time."

Enrolling

Sponsoring your prospect into your business may seem like the culmination of all your prospecting efforts. In reality, it's only the start. This is when your partnership really begins.

Before you can properly support someone, you must first be clear about what you are supporting him to do!

Start by expanding his vision. Help him to write it down in detail as we discussed earlier. Before you begin to train and work with a new distributor INSIST on this as the first step. Without a clear vision for himself and his future in place, your new distributor will never be able to support his new distributors in getting off to the right start. And remember the powerful role vision plays in developing leaders.

You will need to continually remind your people of their vision whenever rejection begins to take its toll, or when their decision to join no longer appears to be such a "convenient" one.

Develop A Detailed Action Plan

For your new distributors to be successful, they must operate from a sound foundation. This includes:

1. Getting trained – in person, by phone, at seminars.

2. Ordering product and support materials.

3. Weekly coaching.

4. Knowing how many people they will need to prospect to achieve their goals.

5. Knowing where to get the names of prospects or how to develop leads.

6. How to build.   And most important ...

7. How to LISTEN!

Chapter Eight

Listening Through Objections

"This sounds like one of those pyramid schemes."

How many times have you heard this objection?

And how many times have you responded with, "Well, it is a network marketing company, but it's certainly not an illegal business," or, "Yes, but our company is different...?" How many hours do you spend researching and memorizing stock, scripted answers to the most common objections? How does it look to your prospect when you turn and with anger or embarrassment react personally to the objection they just presented?

I'm sure you noticed the title of this chapter, "Listening Through Objections?" That's different from overcoming objections – isn't it?

Does your prospect really want you to answer her with your opinion – an opinion that makes her wrong?

Clearly, your opinion may not be worth very much to your prospect.

Countering an objection creates a standoff. You say black and she says white. Who's right? What's more, who's going to be wrong? Do you know something he doesn't? Has anyone ever made you do something or convinced you to do something you didn't want to do? Of course not. Do you appreciate it when someone makes you wrong? Of course not.

Instead, do this: Listen! Listen! Listen!

Listen THROUGH what they're saying to hear how they are thinking and feeling. Their objection voices only part, if any, of their true feelings. The initial response is almost always a smokescreen or a justification for a deeper, more personal fear. Listen for the true concern behind the smoke.

Even the word objection brings up a negative connotation.

Derived from the Latin ob (toward) and jacere (to throw), objection denotes the expression of opposition. Looking at other definitions, you see that an objective is something different. It means something worked for – a goal. Why not look upon objections from this point of view? Use the positive connotation. Something that you can strive for. Look for your prospects to "throw opportunity toward" you, rather than the opposition of objections "at you."

Objections can provide you with an opportunity to create relationships with your prospects by hearing and understanding their feelings, giving them a chance to open up to you.

What a shift to actually encourage your prospects to

have objections! They become opportunities to clear up any falsehoods and develop a sense of belief and trust on the part of your prospects.

Another positive interpretation of objections, is to listen to them as openings, opportunities to shift your prospect's interpretation.

Actually, this is one of your jobs as a network marketer. You get paid to listen through objections.

An interpretation you can take towards objections is that they are the real opportunity. If no one had any objections, then everyone with whom you shared your business would enroll. You would quickly have everyone in the business and that opportunity would be over!

Welcoming objections is part of your job. That's why you get paid 50 percent of the product sales and downline commissions. Can this point of view make the whole concept of objections fun for you?

And the more you practice, the easier and more fun it will get.

The Five Step Process

The process of listening through objections is a powerful way to develop a relationship with people. It can be used in your prospecting for your network marketing business, but also in any conversation where someone may not necessarily agree with your point of view. The process of listening truly honors the values of others, which allows you to better understand who they are. It allows them to vent their frustrations, share their feelings and remain emotionally secure in their communications with you.

And in a world where people are rarely if ever heard, your willingness to truly listen, will attract others to you like a magnet.

Not every conversation you have will end up with your prospect taking action in your favor. Often, the process will take more than one conversation. Some prospects will have deep-seated, complex emotions about a particular subject or point of view, emotions which may take several conversations to communicate to you. You honor others by truly listening to those underlying concerns without demanding anything in return.

Your objective is to have your communication with them be complete. Whether or not your prospect enrolls in your business or evens changes his point of view, as long as you generated an open listening that empowers the other person, you have succeeded in your job.

I learned the following five-step process from the master of listening through objections, Richard Brooke.

Step One: Embrace the Objection

To "embrace," is defined as "to hold in one's arms as a display of affection." What a complete contrast to the usual agree/disagree scenario in a typical "overcoming objections" conversation. To display affection for your prospect through listening and honoring their responses to you, not arguing or being defensive, may seem unnatural to you at first, but try it on and watch what happens.

"I have no time to do another business." Welcome the objection. Don't say, "Yes you do," or, "You don't need much time." These counter the objection like a defensive chess move. Resisting and pushing only invite your prospect to push you back. Get on their side. Agree with them and find out more. Embrace the objection and do it with sincerity.

The objections people give you are concerns they hold as true. And these concerns are very real for them.
"I have no time to do your business." Their plate is full. They're in overwhelm. Frustrated. Working long hours. No time for fun. You know what your business can provide for them – only they know they don't have time to do it.
So, are you going to take their schedule and plan out their day finding enough hours in it so they can do the business? Would you want someone dictating to you what your day should be like?

Remember, push and they will push back. What you resist persists. Don't argue. As I said before, their concerns are real to them. Don't try to fix them, but don't buy into their stories either.

Their stories are not the truth. The degree that you "buy into" their stories and excuses, is the degree to which you are not supporting them being successful and complete in their lives.

So, what is there to do in this embracing business?

Listen to them. Listen through their concern. Develop true empathy. Look them in the eye and simply listen. Shut your mouth (tape is optional) and get into their world. Feel how it is for them. Open your heart and embrace theirs.

How? Hang on, I'm coming to that.
What's important for you to know, is when you connect

with someone in this way, you honor them. They are being truly heard. And when human beings are heard, they will shift and open up to the awesome power of possibilities.

They will begin to show you their heart.

It may not sound like that's what they're doing at first. It may sound like anger. Their voice may be loud. Their intonations may sound harsh.

Just keep your heart open.

The harshness will soften.

They may sound scared. Their tone may project fear.

Keep your heart open. Continue to embrace their words as you proceed to the next step in the process ....

Step Two: Define the Objection

As the person speaks about their concerns, make sure you understand clearly just what the objection is. Asking, "What do you mean by that?" or encouraging them to, "Say more about that," will draw out what they mean.

Don't guess or assume you know what they mean. Be aware of your own listening. If she's talking about not having enough time to do the business, find out how much time she thinks it takes to succeed, or how much time she thinks you spend on the business.

You'll be surprised what people come up with. You may know that to succeed in your business takes a part-time effort of maybe eight to ten hours per week. But your prospect may think the income you are discussing takes a full-time, forty-hours-plus-a-week effort – and they certainly don't have that much time.

Find out. Make sure you know what she's thinking.

Never assume you know what is in her mind. So many enrollments are lost to assumptions and unclear definitions of what others think and feel.

Your job is to contribute the possibility of your opportunity to your prospects. You are listening to see if your business is a fit for them. You are proposing a burden – not a benefit – if your prospect can't fit your business into his schedule. Does he see ways your business can fit into his existing activities? Does he see your business as just another JOB – big effort, little return? Make sure you clearly define the objection fully before you move on to the next step in the process...

Step Three: Embellish the Objection

Embellish means to adorn or make more beautiful (to add fanciful or fictitious details).

Am I really asking you to add details to their objection and make it beautiful?

Yes, I am.

Something to keep in mind as we go through this process, is that network marketing is the antithesis of sales. In traditional sales training you're taught to throw the objection back to your prospect. This leaves all their feelings and concerns associated with the objection in the first place still in place.

This traditional approach only makes people wrong. In essence, it calls your prospect a liar.

What thoughts do you have about someone when they say things to make you sound like a liar? You go away and check out, not physically, but mentally. Your mind goes somewhere nice and pleasant like the Bahamas. It won't stay in a situation where it is being made wrong or being dominated. When you are made wrong, there is no bond between you and the other person – except perhaps antagonism. No connectedness. No friendship.

As you're going through this process, remember that objections, manifested as concerns, have emotions attached to them. These emotions are deeply embedded in a whole body of conversations and experiences from the past that are just waiting to rear their ugly heads. Keep opposing these emotions and they'll get stronger, and probably uglier. They will fight back!

Instead, try something different. Embellish the objection. Make it beautiful. Add to it. Let it be heard, understood and respected.

Keep saying to your prospect, "Say more about that .... What other concerns do you associate with that?" Get all the emotion out. As the definition of embellish says, add fanciful or fictitious details. Make up stories of what it must be like to have the objection.

For example, take the classic "No time" objection. Here's how it goes:

"It sounds like you really don't have any time even to do little things. You probably don't get to read the newspaper or watch the weather forecast on TV do you? Do you have any time for yourself?"

Can you see how this approach validates their objection – and with it, your prospect himself? It connects him with his emotion. It doesn't fight or oppose it.

With this approach, you honor the person's values. They're being heard. How many people do you think have listened to their concerns about not having the time to do what they want recently?

Their thoughts will still be there, but you've created enough space for the emotion to dissipate. And as it does, the feelings shift from negative to positive, and you go on to the next step ....

Step Four: Purging the Objection

The word purge has many definitions: to free from impurities by cleansing; to rid of guilt (or fear); to cause evacuation; to rid of the undesirable.

As you've embellished the objection, and made room for their emotions to come up, there is a moment when all the "bad" stuff is out. Your prospect is purged of the negative emotions associated with the objection. You will actually see a physical change in the person if you are face to face, or you'll hear a change in their voice if you're with them on the telephone.

Their being, who they are at the moment, literally shifts when the purging is complete. A lighter facial expression will be evident. Their body language will loosen up. They could sigh or even laugh out loud. They'll relax.

You are now nearly home free as you move into the next step in the process ...

Step Five: Transition

The transition step is the place where the process changes from one state to another. It is a passage causing a connection to be made between two different themes.
In the transition, you've arrived at the moment in the conversation that you've waited for. The objection has been

purged. All the negative feelings and emotions have gone – at least temporarily – and you now have the opportunity to really connect with your prospect.

The connection takes place in the form of offering the awesome power of possibilities. The most powerful words you could use at this transition – words which actually put your prospect in a state of open, positive emotion – are, "Would you be willing...?" Then share how what you are offering is an opportunity which might fit them.
When you ask, "If I could show you a way around that problem, would you be willing to take a look?" The majority of times the answer will be, "Yes."

Now, you and your prospect are looking at the possibility together. You're on the same side. Connecting two themes. Offering possibilities and seeing if there's a fit.

Remember, what you offer may not be appropriate for her. There may not be a fit. She may not be willing to take that look with you at this point in her life.

However, you have listened, honored, and respected her and left her with a positive impression. You have created an atmosphere of care and concern. Here is the shift in the paradigm where we all get to play a role in creating the new paradigm of network marketing. Listen, honor, respect.

People will begin to respond when you say proudly that this is a network marketing opportunity. You will then see how much of an impact you can truly have on the future of the world!

Chapter Nine

Designing Your Game Plan for Success

It's true, success leaves clues. One of these clues is that whenever people are trying hard and not succeeding, or whenever there is frustration, struggle, or a lack of productivity, one of the missing elements is usually a structure for accomplishment. Simply put, people don't do what's necessary to succeed.

With this in mind, let's take several of the keys to success we've discussed, and look at how we might set up a structure or game plan to achieve your goals.

The problem with conventional goal-setting is the natural tendency we have to avoid it. You operate as though a goal is something you want and don't have. It's set up as an opportunity for suffering.

Suffering is, after all, the feeling you have after spending too long having something you don't want – or wanting something you don't have. Goals have the potential to dominate you. And no one likes to be dominated.

Let's shift your relationship to setting goals. Rather than being attached to the result, I want you to focus on those actions necessary to achieve the result.

Now, you're still committed to your result, but your focus is on your action plan, instead of the negative interpretation you are likely to create if you fall short of your goals. As you focus on your actions, you will be constantly looking for areas in which to develop yourself to be more effective in what you do and how you do it.

You'll be concentrating on Kaizen, a Japanese word describing a process of constant and never-ending improvement. The ever-present question you will use is, "How can I be more effective in my communication and more attractive as a sponsor?"

With this approach you'll look at goal setting as an origin instead of a destination. That way, you can commit yourself to be in personal development or research about who you are being that will empower others to want to join you in partnership.

You might develop your listening for what it is like in the other person's world in order to get a better appreciation for how your opportunity might fill a need and contribute to her. Instead of listening to agree or disagree with someone, you might begin to listen for the value in what they are saying, regardless of how they say it.

Or, perhaps you might develop yourself in the area of listening for how you can create partnership with others, how you can create a bond with them to be a foundation for accomplishment?

You can use the game plan you're designing to develop any number of areas to support your success – be it enrollment, partnering, or other leadership skills.

Wherever you are limited in your business, you are limited in your life. The two are not separate, so your plan affects both. You can integrate the same skills you need for business into your daily life.

Now, what is sure to happen once you've set some goals and a structure for accomplishing them?

Problems. Problems or disruptions show up anytime you make a commitment, such as a business plan.

In our culture, we live in a structure that says that problems are bad, something to be avoided. We are conditioned to interpret problems as signs of something wrong – wrong with us, with others, or with the situation at hand. As a result, we tend to avoid any risk that may contain problems and return to the status quo.

It's also called quitting.

I'm asking you to view problems as interpretations you make up and to shift your relationship to them. Look at them instead as opportunities to take actions to achieve your objectives. Begin to embrace problems as tools for your development in areas which support your success.

Developing Your Plan – Summary

Let's review and bring all of this together.

Based on your overall vision, look at what your income expectations are and your time frame for achieving them.

Start with a six-month schedule. Although your vision will require a more general plan, focus first on your immediate actions.

You'll want to work with your upline leaders to find answers to the following questions:

1. What is the next highest position in your compensation plan, and when will you achieve it?
2. How much earned income do you expect per month, and when do you expect it?
3. How much monthly volume will you need to create in your group to earn that income?
4. How many distributors will you need to partner with to bring this about?
5. What position will you attain by month six, and how much income will it provide?
6. What resources will you need to accomplish that?
   a. Time to invest per week.
   b. Supplies to order, including product and support materials.
   c. Educational and training materials you'll need.
7. Who will work with you to support you?
8. How will you develop your list of prospects? Will you advertise? When and where?
9. What training and development seminars will you attend?
10. Will you build using three-way calling with your upline?
11. Will you build locally and in person, or long distance by fax, phone or the internet?

12. What support structure does your company have for you to use?
13. What will go into your sorting packages?
14. How will you duplicate yourself?
15. What other resources will you need?

Determine a Single Daily Action to Support Your Goals

A single daily action is something you will do consistently and continuously to bring about your success. At minimum, it will include:

- X number of prospecting conversations.
- X number of follow-up conversations.
- X number of packages you'll mail or hand out.
- X number of hours you'll spend on training and coaching your downline.
- Any other action needed, daily, to ensure your success.

How Much is Enough?

To determine how many people you will initially need to prospect, work backwards, starting with your goals. Use input from your upline to "ground" what it will take to reach your target in reality.

Here's an example: IF you generally enroll one out of 20 prospects ..., and IF one prospect out of three builds a business ..., and IF your goal is to find two business-builders each month ..., THEN you will need to prospect 120 people per month to find your two business-builders. IF you work five days per week, THEN you will need to prospect six people each day to reach your objective each month.

Where Will You Get Your Prospects?

If you need 120 prospects each month (continuing the previous example), will you get them from ...

- your warm market of family, friends, and acquaintances?
- ads?
- business or trade shows?
- radio or TV commercials?
- co-op ad programs?
- the Internet?
- other sources?

It's essential that you have enough people to prospect to remain on track toward your goals and to maintain a powerful, productive posture.

What Area of Your Character Will You Develop as You Prospect?

Network marketing is a numbers game only if you don't speak to enough people! Leverage your success by developing yourself. Possible target areas for your development will include:

- Your Listening
- Your Belief
- Your Courage
- Your Persistence

- Your Energy
- Your Communication Skills
- Organization Skills
- Powerful Speaking
- Developing Rapport
- Developing Vision
- Guiding a Conversation
- Not Dumping Information
- Listening for what's important of missing in your prospect's life
- Listening for an opportunity to contribute
- Elements that would make you more attractive as a business partner

Create a Debriefing System

Mike Smith was instrumental in stressing to me the unending necessity for an effective debriefing system. How can you develop yourself if you're not getting any feedback? You begin by establishing a system for getting and using this vital information.

1. Keep a journal

Record the highlights of every conversation. Record the area of yourself you plan to develop. What worked? What was missing? How could you be more effective? How could you listen and communicate more powerfully?

Keep track of your chosen development areas as you prospect. Make at least 100 to 500 calls and rate yourself after each and every one. You'll see tremendous improvement in your effectiveness, and you will be able to put to use everything you learn.

2. Record your calls

Ask one of your mentors to listen to you as you make calls and give you feedback. Also, listen to yourself to hear how you sound to others and make any adjustments necessary.

3. Make three-way calls

Listen in on prospecting calls made by your upline. Then, have your upline listening in on calls you make. Record their feedback, and pay particular attention to those mentors whose skills and techniques consistently get results.

4. Ask your prospects for feedback

That's right! Whether they are interested or not, they are still your audience. You might ask something like, "I'm working on being a more effective communicator. Would you be willing to give me feedback on ... (add your development areas)?"

5. Create your own debriefing structure.

One that works well for me, is to make up a sign that speaks to whatever area I'm working on. I place it by the phone as a continual reminder to smile, shut-up, ask questions, etc.

Constantly Reassess Your Actions

What's working? What's missing? Are you on track? If not, what do you need to realign with your development, your goals, your values or vision? It's critical to always make sure that the actions you take are in line with your intended results. If your results are not what you expected, look to "ground" your action plan in reality to better achieve your goals.

Duplicate It!

Network marketing is always about duplication. Find something that works for you and then go out and teach others how to do it. Keep this in mind as you develop your game plan. If it's not duplicable, it will be of little use to those who follow your leadership.

Chapter Ten

Further Keys to Your Success

Organization

Organization is the cornerstone of successful behavior. Without it, all of your positive actions and achievements become lost in an ineffective hodgepodge of unrelated events.

Although organization manifests itself as an orderly physical game plan to follow, it always begins with your mental clarity. Organization is the result of having researched all of the essential elements needed for success before they are arranged as a detailed, logical progression of events and tasks. Without organization, hard work is only partially effective. With it, the results of your energy and effort become leveraged geometrically as your efficiency increases.

Effectiveness is more a function of focus than of time. This is why it's not enough to only work harder to maximize your effectiveness, but to work smarter as well. This is where the dramatic breakthrough in productivity occurs. This is not to say that putting in the hours is not important, but with focus and constant reflection, each hour will produce optimum results.

Success in network marketing begins with being organized. It means first being trained yourself in all the elements needed to succeed. Then, later on, being able to duplicate this training with your downline.

We spoke earlier of breaking everything down to the lowest common denominator which I've called a single daily action. During the different stages of building your organization, these actions will change in importance and scope. Those tasks needed to attract and work personally with people will give way to management, training and implementing support structures.

In the initial stages of building an organization, it will be necessary to start with building your names list of prospects, prospecting a minimum number of individuals daily, sending out informational packages, following-up, enrolling, training, and doing activities which support your start-up phase. Proper organization will include keeping track of all those with whom you speak. This includes noting all relevant information concerning what's important or missing in their lives, their areas of interest, any objections (and objectives), the end result of the conversation, the next step to take and when to take it, etc.

Let's continue to look at some other qualities which will contribute to your success.

Commitment

Until one is committed there is hesitancy, the chance to draw back, always ineffectiveness.

Concerning all acts of initiative (and creation) there is one elementary truth, the ignorance of which kills countless ideas and splendid plans: That the moment one definitely commits oneself, then Providence moves, too.

All sorts of things occur to help one that would have otherwise never occurred.

A whole stream of events issue from the decision, raising in one's favor all manner of unforeseen incidents and meetings and material assistance, which no man could have dreamt would have come his way.

I have learned a deep respect for one of Goethe's couplets:

"Whatever you can do, or dream you can ... begin it.
Boldness has genius, power and magic in it."
- W.H. Murry
The Scottish Himalayan Expedition, 1951

With commitment, there is no turning back. Your commitment will open up new possibilities that would not reveal themselves to someone with less at stake.

Commitment means doing whatever it takes to make a way to succeed. Contrast this with how most people enter into a decision – and particularly the decision to build a network marketing organization. For most people, it may sound appealing, promising, or like a good idea. In other words, it shows up like a "convenient" thing to do.

However, when someone makes such a decision of convenience to join a networking organization – as opposed to a commitment to do it no matter what – their entire relationship to the process is very different. What may appear convenient today may not be convenient tomorrow. There is nothing like rejection to derail someone who is not fully committed to doing whatever it takes to succeed.

The key to succeeding in network marketing is to operate, day in and day out, out of your commitment to your action plan, your goals and your vision – not out of reaction to your feelings. Most people are at the mercy of their feelings, that is, if they feel like making their calls they do, and if they do not feel like it, they do not. Unfortunately there are too many factors which may cause you to not feel like doing what is essential to benefit your business on a daily basis.

The answer then is to be clear about what is at stake and what you are committed to doing and, whether you feel like it or not, honor your commitment to yourself and your plan and do it anyway. As you train yourself to regularly return to your commitment you will be building strength in the muscle that will launch your business powerfully forward.

Let me share with you a tale about commitment and playing with something significant at stake.

Sometimes commitment can be a life and death decision. In 1987, Dennis Pezzolesi had just graduated from dental school and had a promising career ahead of him. Unfortunately, he was about to self-destruct.

In 1988, he endured a bitter divorce, which left him financially broken and led to a drinking problem. In 1992, he was involved in a drunk driving accident, which killed the driver of the other car, a man named Renford Gilling. The accident was a tragedy for a couple of reasons. For one thing, it took the life of another man. And two, it led to a series of events which could have left Dennis feeling sorry for himself while giving up any hope of ever living a productive life.

Following the accident, Pezzolesi lost his job. Being already financially strapped, he soon found himself in bankruptcy. His punishment was jail time plus 3000 hours of community service – leaving him little time to start up his own practice and earn a decent living. With a new wife and child to support, Dennis was at a crossroads. He could either give up or fight back.

Around this same time, Dennis' dental school roommate introduced him to network marketing. He saw early on – from the people he met and the value-based leadership his company provided – that his life had value and his story had the potential to inspire thousands. Although the timing could not have been worse to dedicate to this type of business, Dennis saw this for what it was – the opportunity of a lifetime. Despite all of the challenges he was facing in his life, he decided to commit to building his network marketing business with laser focus. This commitment has resulted in a growing worldwide organization, securing the financial future of his family.

Dennis is also using his story to inspire others while contributing to their lives. Through the personal development work he has undertaken while building his network marketing business, he has summoned up the courage from within to tell others about the dangers of drinking and driving, thus honoring Renford Gilling. Without an unwavering commitment to his family, his business and his life, there may have been two lives lost in that tragic accident.

Enthusiasm

Enthusiasm comes from the Greek word meaning the spirit-force within. There is no substitute for enthusiasm – that i-a-s-m, "I Am Sold Myself" quality that causes a person to radiate positive energy which attracts others like a magnet.

Enthusiastic people want to be around other positive enthusiastic people. As a result, those who give off these "vibrations" find themselves surrounded by other enthusiastic leaders.

Not all enthusiastic people are leaders, but all charismatic leaders possess this quality. It is impossible to achieve all that you are capable of achieving if you do not love what you do, if you do not possess the spirit within. The key to enthusiasm is being able to choose what you do. If it's a struggle, a "should," or an obligation, you won't be able to generate this enthusiastic force of attraction. Hard work without enthusiasm leads to drudgery, boredom, and resentment.

Instead, create an interpretation that allows you to choose everything you do – then, the enthusiasm will flow. If you're not in a place of choice about something, choose differently. Choose not to do it.

But enthusiasm alone is not enough. It must be combined with focus and the commitment to implement your action plan. Without being matched to appropriate actions, enthusiasm is just a good idea. When enthusiasm and actions combine, your words, tone, and gestures will possess extra spark to ignite other people's passion.

Enthusiasm works to magnify the results of your actions. It brings out the best in people and enables you to empower others to their greatness.

Persistence

Let me tell you a story.

There was once a skilled stone cutter working diligently with his sledge hammer on a huge boulder lying at the mouth of a path through the forest. People gathered to watch him swing and swing, attempting to split the stone.

After several dozen swings without results, some observers grew tired of watching and moved on. After a hundred swings without so much as a chip, others began to snicker and taunt the stone cutter. As he persevered, people would laugh and call him crazy to work so hard with nothing to show for his efforts.

Through 200, then 300, then 400 swings, the stone cutter continued to swing away, undaunted by the growing number of derisive onlookers.

Finally, on his 500th swing, the stone split exactly where the stone cutter wanted, cleanly and in two pieces-much to the astonishment of the crowd.

The result, however, was no surprise to the stone cutter. He knew his persistent effort would eventually succeed.

Persistence is essential to a networker's success. Lack of perseverance in the face of adversity and discouragement separates those who succeed from those who quit. This persistence is fueled by the commitment to do whatever it requires to see a positive result come from what may, at that moment, appear to be futile. It is the solid, unshakable belief in one's ultimate success that fuels this commitment to persevere.

This quality of persistence combined with the willingness to constantly look for what's missing and to adapt to what is necessary in order to succeed is a trait shared by all successful distributors. Persistence does not mean doing the same thing over and over, expecting success to come from an unending string of identical failures. Doing the same things repeatedly while expecting different results is one definition of what it means to be crazy.

With the support of your mentors, and by duplicating behaviors that have been proven successful, persistence will ultimately triumph. Never forget to look for what's working and what's missing. Ask yourself, "How can I better leverage my actions to bring about my intended results?"

Vision

Every accomplishment, without exception, can be traced back to someone's idea. All goals are consistent with a series of actions that were necessary to achieve them. All action follows thought. It is the combination of both individual and group visions that produces results.

As we've discussed, one of the keys to success in network marketing is the ability to clearly focus on your vision, your reason for involvement. Without having mastered the ability to clearly and specifically record all of the elements of your vision, it would be impossible to support someone else to do the same.

The skill of asking the appropriate questions to help clarify another person's vision is a critical step in developing commitment.

Questions like:

"What would you do with an extra $5,000, $10,000, or $20,000 per month?"

"How would this opportunity change your life?"

"What would you do – or no longer do – once you gained financial freedom?"

"How would you contribute to others if you had more money than you could ever spend?"

"To whom would you contribute?"

"What childhood dreams have you given up?"

"What would you do if you no longer needed to work for a living?"

"Would you continue to work?"

Ask yourself these questions, and you will find it easy to generate thought-provoking questions to ask others. Become proficient in "dream weaving" and you'll have more people around you than the Pied Piper of Hamelin.

Holding and living your vision is an essential part of living with passion – and living with passion is what creates an unending stream of the awesome power of possibilities in your life.

Living Your Values and Honoring Others' Values

Passion and vision intertwine when your actions are firmly rooted in your values. Your values link who you are with what you do.

As Carol McCall of the World Institute Group teaches, values are codes of honor and the essence of who people really are. Values form the fabric of your soul. They are the thread of integrity which cannot be pulled. When people's values are violated, they become angry, noncommunicative, or withdrawn. Values demand to be honored.

Once you begin to consciously identify your values, you can seek to relate how these values are manifested in your life and in the lives of others. Combining actions with values connects a person to the essence of his inner vitality and outward activity. The result is empowered productivity with real velocity and balanced harmony.

The following list is a sampling of possible core values you may have:

Acceptance	Freedom
Joy	Recognition
Appreciation	Harmony
Relationship	Order
Belonging	Honesty
Participation	Respect
Comfort	Humor
Peace	Safety
Communication	Independence
Perfection	Security
Integrity	Pleasure
Spirituality/God	Creativity
Intimacy	Power
Trust	Work

- Adapted from the
"Design Your Life Workshop Manual" The World Institute Group

One of the essential skills each networking leader will need to develop is supporting others in recognizing which values are of top priority for them, and then designing a life in accordance with these values.

Knowing and living your values by planning and completing goals that honor those values is essential to developing the self-motivation so important to your networking success. As Richard Brooke teaches, self-motivation relies on expectation. If you expect to succeed, your actions will naturally synchronize with your expectation.

You must be in a position of choice about what you do. That's why you can't make anyone take part in network marketing if they do not freely choose to do so.

The most successful leaders succeed because their efforts and actions are an extension of who they are. While they are committed to achieving the results they expect, they are not attached to these results. They do not label themselves or their actions as failures if they do not reach their goals on the schedule they set. Instead, they simply refocus on their actions and put in place whatever was missing which is needed to bring about the desired result.

Leaders who operate from this inner passion in which their work is synonymous with play, love the process as much – and often more – than they do the end result. That's what makes them so powerful and effective. They work out of a natural love for what they do, with no one to please but themselves. The satisfying pursuit of what they love to do translates into success for themselves and a duplication of that same success as they contribute this gift to others.

Chapter Eleven

The Gift of Network Marketing

According to Greek mythology, there once lived a sad and lonely king on the island of Cyprus. He was alone. He did not relate well to women. He was a great sculptor. One day he set out to create a sculpture of a beautiful woman. Putting all his heart and soul into this work, he succeeded in creating an incredibly beautiful statue – so beautiful that he fell deeply in love with his own marble creation.

Plagued by an even greater loneliness and longing than before, he prayed to Aphrodite, goddess of love, to grant his wish that his sculpture come to life.

Out of the king's great love for this woman of stone, and with the help of Aphrodite who took pity on the lovelorn king, the sculpture of the woman did indeed come alive.

The king's name was Pygmalion. And the Pygmalion Effect, is the term used to describe the life-altering power of positive expectations.

Russ DeVan, president of Success by Design, frequently cites another example of the Pygmalion Effect. It can be found in "The Wizard of Oz." Throughout the movie, the principle characters search desperately for qualities they already possess. The Scarecrow wants a brain, the Tin Man a heart, the Lion courage. And Dorothy wants to go home. We watch the Scarecrow make decisions about what to do and where to go.

The Tin Man cries with emotion and feeling so often, he has to carry an oil can to treat his tear-rusted joints. The Cowardly Lion repeatedly risks his life for his friends. And Dorothy finds, at last, that all she ever needed to do was click her heels together and wish to be home in Kansas.

But the characters don't know of their true abilities until the little dog Toto reveals the true identity of the Wizard.

As the Wizard presents the Scarecrow with a diploma, he recites the Pythagorean Theorem and the straw-man realizes his new-found intelligence.

The Tin Man, receiving his heart-shaped clock, feels his heart breaking at the prospect of leaving his friends.

The Lion receives a Medal of Honor to signify his courage, and it transforms him from a whiny coward into King of Beasts.

Likewise, with the knowledge that she can actually make it happen herself, Dorothy sees she can return home simply by clicking her heels and willing it to be so.

In reality, nothing changed for any of them. All four characters are transformed by the belief that the Wizard instilled in them.

They now have the power of expectation.
They now believe in the awesome power of possibilities.

This is the gift network marketing can be: to transform the lives of people into their dreams and to make their expectations real.

As you communicate your vision of possibilities and inspire people to create their own powerful visions, lives are altered. Your ability to bring out the best in others by communicating your belief in them can propel them beyond their previous expectations.

This is the Awesome Power of Possibilities. With the realization of your ability to truly empower and affect the lives of people, you can transform not only given individuals, but the entire culture as well.

This is the challenge. And I invite you ... encourage you to take it on. Create for others and yourself the inspiration required to design and then live an ideal life of choice in which anything is possible.

This is the possibility that network marketing offers. It goes far beyond financial and time and personal freedom. It creates awesome possibilities for people in all aspects of their relationships and their lives.

Is this a possibility for you?

Go ahead. Be your own Wizard. Pull away the curtain and watch the miracles show up all around you – and the world will be filled with the Awesome Power of Your Possibilities.

Dr. Joe Rubino is widely acknowledged as one of North America's foremost success and productivity coaches. He is the CEO of Visionary International Partnerships. To date, more than 500,000 people have benefited from his coaching and leadership development training. Together with Dr. Tom Ventullo, he is the co-founder of The Center For Personal Reinvention, an organization that provides coaching and productivity and leadership development courses that champion people to maximize their personal power and effectiveness.

Also by Dr. Joe Rubino:
- *The Power to Succeed: 30 Principles for Maximizing Your Personal Effectiveness*
- *The Power to Succeed: More Principles for Powerful Living, Book II,*
- *The Magic Lantern: A Fable About Leadership, Personal Excellence and Empowerment*
- *Secrets of Building A Million Dollar Network Marketing Organization from A Guy Who's Been There, Done That and Shows You How to Do It Too.*
- *10 Weeks to Network Marketing Success: The Secrets to Launching Your Very Own Million-Dollar Organization in A 10-Week Business-Building and Personal-Development Self-Study Course (6 audio cassettes and workbook)*
- *Restore Your Magnificence: A Life-Changing Guide to Reclaiming Your Self-Esteem*

To request information about any of The Center For Personal Reinvention's programs or to order any of Dr. Rubino's books, visit http://www.CenterForPersonalReinvention.com

Recommended Personal Development Programs

The Center For Personal Reinvention
Dr. Joe Rubino and Dr. Tom Ventullo

Where are you blocked in your life and in your business?
Where is there an unacceptable level of resignation or conflict?
Where are there interpersonal listening and communications skills
lacking?
Where are you lacking partnership, commitment and vision?

The world we live and work in is marked by unprecedented
change and fraught with new and complex challenges. For many of
us, life begins to look like an uphill struggle to survive instead of a
fun and exciting opportunity to grow, risk, and live your dreams in
partnership with others. The stresses, conflicts and frustrations we
experience daily need not be so.

There exists another possibility.

…To live and work with passion -- empowered by the challenges of
life.
…To champion others to achieve excellence in a nurturing environ-
ment that fosters partnerships.
…To acquire the success principles that support mutuality, creativity
and harmony.
…To take on the art of listening and communicating in such a way
that others are impacted to see new possibilities for accomplishment,
partnership and excellence.

Reinventing ourselves, our relationships and our perception of
the world is the result of a never-ending commitment to our own personal magnificence and to that of others. It is made possible through
acquiring approximately 50 key principles that cause people to begin
to view life and people in an entirely different way. When people really
get these principles, life, relationships, and new possibilities for
breakthroughs show up from a totally fresh perspective. Through the

use of cutting-edge technology as a vibrant basis for learning, growing and acting, The Center For Personal Reinvention successfully supports people to view life with a new and fresh awareness as they self-discover these life-changing principles.

With this program, YOU will:

- Uncover the secrets to accessing your personal power while maximizing your productivity.
- Gain clarity on exactly what it will take to reach your goals with velocity.
- Create a structure for skyrocketing your effectiveness while developing new and empowering partnerships.
- Learn how taking total responsibility for every aspect of your life and business can result in breakthrough performance.
- Discover the key elements of a detailed action plan and how to reach your goals in record time.
- Acquire the keys to listening and communicating effectively and intentionally.
- Recognize and shift out of self-defeating thoughts and actions.
- Gain the insight to better understand others with new compassion and clarity.
- Learn how to develop the charisma necessary to attract others to you.
- Experience the confidence and inner peace that comes from stepping into leadership.

The Center for Personal Reinvention
...Transferring the Power to Succeed!

Customized Courses and Programs Personally Designed For Achieving Maximum Results

Areas of Focus include:

Designing Your Future
Making Life and Businesses Work
Generating Infinite Possibilities

Creating Conversations for Mutuality
Commitment Management
Personal Coaching and Development
Maximizing Personal Effectiveness
Breakthrough Productivity
Leadership Development
Relationship and Team Building
Conflict Resolution
Listening for Solutions
Systems for Personal Empowerment
Personal and Productivity Transformation
Designing Structures for Accomplishment
Creating Empowered Listening Styles
Possibility Thinking
Forwarding Action
Structures for Team Accountability
Innovative Thinking
Completing with The Past
Creating A Life of No Regrets

The Center For Personal Reinvention champions companies and individuals to achieve their potential through customized programs addressing specific needs consistent with their vision for the future. Contact us today to explore how we might impact your world!

The Center For Personal Reinvention
PO Box 217,
Boxford, MA 01921
drjrubino@email.com
Tel: (888) 821-3135
Fax: (630) 982-2134

Personal and Group Coaching Programs
The Value of Coaching to Support Your Business and Your Life

In our daily lives as well as in our businesses, we typically deal with life's challenges the best we know how. If we knew what it would take to be more effective in our relationships, more productive in our activities or more successful in reaching our goals, we would surely change accordingly. The only access we ordinarily have to impact our lives comes from the areas of "what we know" and "what we don't know." In our efforts to achieve more, we usually resort to increasing what we do know by learning to do things a little better, a little differently or we simply do more of a behavior that produced a certain result for us in the past. This behavior can produce small, incremental increases in our ability to impact our business and our world. Likewise, by educating ourselves in the arena of "what we don't know," this knowledge then becomes part of what we now do know: If you are computer illiterate and you learn how to adeptly operate a computer, you will have successfully converted something that you do not know into what you now know. More than 95 percent of our efforts are spent in these two arenas – what we know and what we don't know.

However, our most extraordinary growth comes from outside the arena of what we know or don't know. This composes the vast variety of ideas that we are blind to, not knowing that they even exist. It's in this arena of "what we don't know we don't know" that breakthroughs occur.

So how do you gain access to this fertile territory if you don't even know that it exists? The answer lies in recruiting the help of a coach who can support you to explore this rich domain that is outside of your customary perspective and behaviors. Your coaches should be individuals who possess the key principles that make them powerful in the particular arena they offer coaching. A coach may be powerful in some arenas but not necessarily in others. The same person who is qualified to coach you in business matters may be totally unqualified to coach you in the area of relationships or spiritual matters. True coaches do not give advice or lend their opinions. They are value based, not ego based. They do not manipulate or exploit to carry out their own agenda. They are totally nonjudgmental. They are not the same as counselors or therapists. They do not try to protect, control or rescue those they are coaching. They instead listen for where you may be experiencing challenges or may be missing some key element that, if put into place, would produce a desired change. Coaches support us in seeing something that we may not be aware of by listening both to what we say and to what we leave out. They empathize with the person being coached, but are not emotionally attached to an outcome. They serve to champion people to have their lives work optimally. They do this by asking questions, exploring possibilities, making requests and, at times, confronting issues that may need to be examined. Skilled coaching is a fine art and a highly valuable service. For a coaching relationship to be possible, there must exist an open willingness on the part of the person being coached to endure and actively participate in the process. Of course, total confidentiality must exist to allow for the freedom to explore any and all areas necessary. The absence of judging and advice creates the opening needed to fully examine any possibility.

Coaching is typically undertaken in any of six major areas of life: business/career, health, wealth, relationships, spirituality/personal development or recreation/passions. A good coach will clarify if his or her coaching client is open to explore any or all of these areas or if the coaching relationship is agreed to be limited to any one or more areas. True coaches are value based and interact with honor and respect while, at the same time, they are not reluctant to call someone on their "stuff" out of a solid commitment to champion the person's excellence and best interests.

Successful coaches:
- Listen for what may be missing to accomplish a result or honor a person's values.
- Lead by example and champion others to step into leadership.
- Are committed to their client's excellence and, at the same time, not attached to his or her responses.
- Are grounded in value-based personal development principles.

- Hold those they coach as totally capable and competent while looking for what might be missing for them to fully experience their magnificence.
- Nurture the person coached to be their best and live with passion while accomplishing their goals.
- Never make the person coached feel small or dependent.
- Champion the person coached to be the best they can be while staying "invisible" as a coach. The coach's ego must not be a factor in the relationship.
- Tell the truth and do not step over uncomfortable topics or situations in order to avoid discomfort or look good.
- Create a safe atmosphere that allows the client to be vulnerable and open to possibilities.
- Support their coaching clients in an accountability structure, ensuring that they follow through on what they say they will do.
- Support the free flow of ideas and conversations for possibilities through idea streaming.

It is helpful for any coaching relationship to begin by developing clarity with respect to the client's overall vision. This vision should include every aspect of the person's life and business. From this wide-ranging perspective, it is then possible to develop a plan to accomplish any goals. These goals blend into the big picture by fulfilling or working toward one aspect of the vision's realization.

A productive coaching relationship can focus on either a life or business project. In the realm of business or network marketing, a coaching relationship is often best undertaken within the context of a project or action plan that is grounded in time. By focusing on producing specific and measurable results, a coach can support a client to best work through any business stops or life challenges en route to the accomplishment of one's goals. A coach can also assist in gaining clarity on all conditions of satisfaction that may be important to a project's fulfillment. Such conditions might include those non-measurable items that would need to take place for a project to be considered a success. These might include developing stronger relationships with family members, spending quality time with children, devoting a minimum amount of time daily to meeting one's own needs, taking a well deserved vacation, etc.

Many people mistakenly assume that they can be successful in business without being successful in other areas of their lives. While important, our businesses are only one component of our lives. If there is an imbalance in any of the six prominent areas of our lives, any business accomplishment will be somehow incomplete. For this reason, a good coach will support a client to adopt a whole-thinking perspective with mastery of all areas of life as the ultimate goal. For this reason, personal development is an essential component of any business coaching relationship. As one undertakes the personal improvement process, increased business productivity will surely result.

Just as an Olympic athlete in pursuit of a gold medal would not think of undertaking such an accomplishment without the support of a coach, most people would likewise benefit from a coaching relationship. Coaching can add fun and excitement to every aspect of your life as you take on the challenge of reinventing yourself and your business, always in search of excellence. And of course, one of the major benefits of an ongoing coaching relationship is that you will develop the coaching skills yourself that will be necessary for you to impact the lives of others, who will likewise look to you for coaching. If you are in business and do not yet have a coach who is committed to championing your success, I strongly encourage you to look into how such a relationship might support your goals and move your business and life forward with velocity.

Hire a Coach

The Center for Personal Reinvention offers network marketing training and individual and group coaching programs that support people to realize their business and life goals while designing a life of choice and without regrets. For more information on hiring a coach, please contact Dr. Joe Rubino at DrJRubino@email.com or by calling (888) 821-3135. To subscribe to the Center for Personal Reinvention Ezine list, send a message to cprsuccess-subscribe@yahoogroups.com

Other Books and Tapes by Dr. Joe Rubino

The Power to Succeed:
30 Principles for Maximizing Your Personal Effectiveness

What exactly distinguishes those who are effective in their relationships, productive in business and happy, powerful and successful in their approach to life from those who struggle, suffer and fail? That is the key question that *The Power to Succeed: 30 Principles for Maximizing Your Personal Effectiveness* supports readers to explore in life-changing detail. The information, examples, experiences and detailed exercises offered will produce life altering insights for readers who examine who they are being on a moment to moment basis that either contributes to increasing their personal effectiveness, happiness and power -- or not. As you commit to an inquiry around what it takes to access your personal power, you will gain the tools to overcome any challenges or limiting thoughts and behavior and discover exactly what it means to be the best you can be.

With this book YOU will:
- Uncover the secrets to accessing your personal power.
- Create a structure for maximizing your effectiveness with others.
- Learn to take total responsibility for everything in your life.
- Discover the key elements to accomplishment and how to reach your goals in record time.
- Identify your life rules and discover how honoring your core values can help you maximize productivity.
- Complete your past and design your future on purpose.
- Discover the keys to communicating effectively and intentionally.
- Stop complaining and start doing.
- Seize your personal power and conquer resignation in your life.
- Learn how to generate conversations that uncover new possibilities.
- See how embracing problems can lead to positive breakthroughs in life.
- Leave others whole while realizing the power of telling the truth.
- Learn how to develop the charisma necessary to attract others to you

The Power to Succeed, Book II:
More Principles for Powerful Living

This revealing book continues where *The Power to Succeed: 30 Principles for Maximizing Your Personal Effectiveness* left off with more powerful insights into what it takes to be most happy, successful and effective with others.

With this book YOU will:
- Discover the keys to unlock the door to success and happiness.
- Learn how your listening determines what you attract to you.
- And how to shift your listening to access your personal power.
- See how creating a clear intention can cause miracles to show up around you.
- Learn the secrets to making powerful requests to get what you want from others.
- Discover how to fully connect with and champion others to realize their greatness.
- Learn to create interpretations that support your excellence and avoid those that keep you small.
- Develop the power to speak and act from your commitments.
- See how communication with others can eliminate unwanted conditions from your life.
- Discover the secret to being happy and eliminating daily upsets.
- Learn how to put an end to gossip and stop giving away your power.
- Develop the ability to lead your life with direction and purpose and discover what it's costing you not to do so.
- And More!!

The Power to Succeed: 30 Principles for Maximizing Your Personal Effectiveness and its sequel, *The Power to Succeed, Book II: More Principles for Powerful Living* are a powerful course in becoming the person you wish to be. Read these books, take on the success principles discussed and watch your life and business transform and flourish.

The Magic Lantern: A Fable About Leadership, Personal Excellence and Empowerment

Set in the magical world of Center Earth, inhabited by dwarves, elves, goblins and wizards, *The Magic Lantern* is a tale of personal development that teaches the keys to success and happiness. This fable examines what it means to take on true leadership while learning to become maximally effective with everyone we meet.

Renowned personal development trainer, coach and veteran author, Dr. Joe Rubino tells the story of a group of dwarves and their young leader who go off in search of the secrets to a life that works, a life filled with harmony and endless possibilities and void of the regrets and upsets that characterize most people's existence. With a mission to restore peace and harmony to their village in turmoil, the characters overcome the many challenges they encounter along their eventful journey. Through self-discovery, they develop the principles necessary to be the best that they can be as they step into leadership and lives of contribution to others.

The Magic Lantern teaches us such noble lessons as:
- the power of forgiveness
- the meaning of responsibility and commitment
- what leadership is really all about
- the magic of belief and positive expectation
- the value of listening as an art
- the secret to mastering one's emotions and actions
- and much more.

It combines the spellbinding story telling reminiscent of Tolkien's *The Hobbit* with the personal development tools of the great masters.

Restore Your Magnificence:
A Life-Changing Guide to Reclaiming Your Self-Esteem

This book is the definitive guide to re-establishing your self-image. Dr. Joe Rubino takes you step-by-step through the same exercises he has used to transform thousands of lives. The easy-to-understand exercises will become your roadmap to a life of happiness, fulfillment and self-esteem.

With this book YOU will:
- Uncover the source of your lack of self-esteem
- Complete the past and stop the downward spiral of self-sabotage
- Replace negative messages with new core beliefs that support your happiness and excellence
- Realize the secret to reclaiming your personal power
- See how you can be strong and authentic. Use your vulnerability as a source of power
- Design a new self-image that supports your magnificence
- Realize the power of forgiveness
- Discover the secret to un upset-free life
- Re-establish your worth and reinvent yourself to be your best
- Create a vision of a life of no regrets

"I have personally used this program's principles to support thousands of people to be self-confident, happy and prosperous. You owe it to yourself to read this book."

– Dr. Tom Ventullo
President, The Center for Personal Reinvention

10 Weeks to Network Marketing Success:
The Secrets to Launching Your Very Own Million-Dollar Organization
in a 10-Week Business-Building and Personal-Development Self-Study Course

Learn the business-building and personal-development secrets that will put you squarely on the path to network marketing success. *10 Weeks to Network Marketing Success* is a powerful course that will grow your business with velocity and change your life!

With this course, YOU will:
- Learn exactly how to set up a powerful 10-week action plan that will propel your business growth.
- Learn how to prospect your most productive niche markets.
- Discover your most effective pathways to success.
- Learn how to persuasively influence your prospects by listening to contribute value.
- Build your business rapidly by making powerful requests.
- Discover the secret to acting from your commitments.
- Create a powerful life-changing structure for personal development.
- See the growth that comes from evaluating your progress on a regular basis.
- Learn how listening in a new and powerful way will skyrocket your business.
- Uncover the secret to accepting complete responsibility for your business.
- Learn how to transform problems into breakthroughs.
- Develop the charisma that allows you to instantly connect with others on a heart-to-heart level.
- Identify the secrets to stepping into leadership and being the source of your success.
- And much more!

The *10-Weeks to Network Marketing Success* Program contains 10 weekly exercises on 6 audio cassettes plus a 37-page workbook.

SECRET #1 - SELF MOTIVATION
Thought Modification Made Easy Audio Cassette Tape Series

Utilize The Latest in Whole Brain Inner Talk™ Technology to take a trip to a deeper dimension of power within yourself and tap into The Most Important Secret To Success In Network Marketing...SELF-MOTIVATION !

Put to work for you the powerful combination of the latest in patented and scientifically proven audible and subliminal brain wave technology developed by Dr. Eldon Taylor, the world's foremost expert on offsetting negative information by inputting positive messages directly into the subconscious. This safe and highly effective proven technology has been independently researched at leading institutions such as Stanford University. For the first time ever, this technology has been combined with the 124 thought altering positive self talk affirmations developed by Dr. Joe Rubino, one of North America's foremost business trainers and coaches. The result is a remarkable audio-cassette tape series that will give you the power to alter any limiting thoughts...The power to maximize your personal effectiveness to rapidly build your network marketing business on purpose and with confidence.

This revolutionary two tape set consists of one Positive Self-Talk Program, which combines audible affirmations with the shadowed subliminal Inner Talk® affirmations, and one Ozo self-motivation program. Use the first tape at least once a day playing it in the background in your car or while you work or play. Use the second tape with headphones when you can take 20 minutes and close your eyes. The special frequencies will entrain brain wave activity and produce an optimal state for learning and conditioning new patterns, energizing you into action and filling your being with total confidence. It's like hiring Dr. Joe Rubino as your personal success coach!

Check your local bookstore or order directly from us.
ORDER COUPON

Yes, I want to invest in my future!
Please send me the following books or tapes by Dr. Joe Rubino.

Books	Price	Qty.	Subtotal
The Power to Succeed: *30 Principles for Maximizing* *Your Personal Effectiveness*	$15.95		
The Power to Succeed, Book II: *More Principles for Powerful Living*	$15.95		
The Magic Lantern: A Fable About Leadership, *Personal Excellence and Empowerment*	$15.95		
Secrets of Building A Million Dollar Network *Marketing Organization from A Guy Who's Been* *There, Done That And Shows You How to Do It Too.*	$17.95		
10-Weeks to Network Marketing Success (6 audio tapes plus workbook)	$69.95		
Secret #1: Self-Motivation (2 audio-tapes)	$39.95		
Restore Your Magnificence: A Life-Changing Guide *to Reclaiming Your Self-Esteem*	$15.95		
MA residents add 5% sales tax			
Shipping and Handling ($4.95 for the first book plus $2 each additional book; $9.95 per book for non-US/Canadian orders)			
QUANTITY DISCOUNTS AVAILABLE		Total	

Name _____ Address _____
City _____ State _____ Zip _____
Email_____ Telephone _____

I'd like to pay by:
☐ Credit Card   Circle one: MasterCard   VISA   American Express
　　Credit Card Number _____ Exp. Date _____
　　Signature _____

☐ Check or Money Order Enclosed (US Funds Only)
　　Please place this order form with payment into an envelope and mail to:
　　Vision Works Publishing　　Or To Order:　Call: (888) 821-3135
　　PO Box 217　　　　　　　　　　　　　　Fax: (630) 982-2134
　　Boxford, MA 01921　　　　　　　　　　Email: VisionWorksBooks@Email.com

☐ I am interested in learning more about The Center For Personal Reinvention's
programs including coaching services.